STOP
OVERTHINKING

"In a moment of decision, the best thing you can do is the right thing to do, the next best thing is the wrong thing, and the worst thing you can do is nothing."

Theodore Roosevelt

BOOKS BY BRIAN LEADER

STOP

OVERTHINKING

Learn Through Mindfulness Meditation and Positive Self-Talk How to Declutter Your Life from Stress, Anxiety, and Negative Thinking, Which Hold Your Mind Stuck in Procrastination

Brian J. Leader

Stop Overthinking

2021 Second Edition
Hardcover Color ISBN: 978-1-8383641-8-2

Book Editing by
Carlos Miguélez

Graphic Design and Professional Typesetting by
TheEarthDesigners™

BRIAN LEADER BOOKS

Table of Contents

Chapter 1.   Introduction

Most people, at some point in life, have found themselves engaging in too much thinking about a particular thing or situation. Overthinking is experiences replaying them repeatedly and, more often than not, dwelling on thoughts and things that have happened or are about to happen. Overthinking is irritating to the mind and can result in serious consequences to an individual's life.

Incessant worrying is overthinking about what could happen. When overthinking starts to affect the mental and emotional part of an individual, then he or she needs to consider getting professional assistance.

Dwelling on thoughts that are not going away will generally affect the well-being of an individual, his or her normal functioning in life, and result in the development of several illnesses. Mental illnesses such as anxiety disorders, panic disorders, trauma, phobias, and bipolar disorders, among others, can cause one to have no control over the rushing thoughts in their minds. Some experiences in life can also lead to overthinking.

Factors That Influence Overthinking

Regrets

Regretting a word or wrong action leads to such an individual replaying the scenario repeatedly. The victim can overthink about diverse outcomes of such a scenario. When people make mistakes, it is obvious that they feel bad about them, but it is equally important to know that no one can change the past. So knowing how to shake off the past is important in ensuring that one remains with a sound mind even after a mistake.

Pressure for performance probably at work

Everyone wants to leave an excellent impression. However, working towards that excellence has nothing to do with a collection of overloaded thoughts. The anxiety of whether one will measure up to the quality standard will only create an unhealthy mind that will be incapable of working towards excellence. When there is the desire to perform, a relaxed mind is the best platform that can absorb new methods, techniques, and information to adapt to for excellence.

The fear of the unknown

Some people are just too creative and can imagine non-existing disasters. The fear that something bad might happen can only be fought through conquering such thoughts with other positive thoughts. Fear can affect the thinking of a victim and place them in a difficult situation of overthinking. When such victims detect such thoughts as they set in, they should discard them to help to save their minds from overthinking.

Obsessive thoughts

Whatever the subject of the thoughts, obsessive thinking can lead to overthinking. This can subsequently lead to an unhealthy state of mind. Obsessive thinking can be because of waiting for an interview, a date, or a performance. A victim can be caught up in too much thinking about what to say, do, or how things will turn out. Thinking too much about such things during such scenarios has negative results. The mind is always overloaded and performs poorly. Obsessive thinking can result in a serious disorder known as obsessive-compulsive disorder.

Fear of worse scenarios

Fear of worst scenarios such as illness can cause overthinking to individuals. When one has health problems, for example, the fear of the worst is likely to come to mind from time to time. When this becomes a constant fear in the mind of the victim, then overthinking sets in. However, this can be avoided by putting necessary measures in place. Learning to avoid such thoughts can also save the health of the person from deteriorating due to the impact of overthinking.

Chapter 2.   Defining Overthinking

In a lesson to do with eliminating overthinking, it is a smart idea to begin with understanding what overthinking really is. How do we do it? Why? There are benefits to analyzing a situation, and even for imagining a worst-case scenario, but go too far, and you are creating a volatile and dangerous mix. Overthinking can be fatal.

First, look at what being an over-thinker is like and if you might be an individual who overthinks, too. There are natural reasons that trigger you to overthink, but there are harmful learned behaviors that cause you to grind yourself down with worry and anxiety. Get a sense of whether or not you overthink, and why.

Determine If You Overthink

Imagine you are waking up in the morning. Maybe it's Wednesday. Maybe you did not get much sleep to begin with because your mind was racing with thoughts all night. Your eyes open. You recall what day this is, and what that means in terms of obligations. Then, suddenly, that trickling thought of today's obligations turns into a raging torrent of thoughts. Everything you were thinking about last night, additional thoughts and worries, and soon it feels in your chest as if you might be drowning.

It is a paralyzing feeling. The lack of taking action compounds your feelings, and now you experience guilt for not taking action. You feel doubt about the choices you might make. You become critical and even cruel to yourself. This vicious little whirlpool gains momentum as you put more thought, worry, energy toward it. It spins in one place, moving fast but going nowhere except deeper into the waters. It is exhausting and even frightening, and you have not even risen from your bed yet.

As you go through the motions of your morning routine, your mind is somewhere else. In the shower, you move through step 1: wash step 2: rinse, step 3: repeat, but your mind is focusing acutely on what was said to you last night. What does it mean? What does it really mean? What you should have said in response. What might have happened if you said what you should have? What might have happened if you did not say anything at all?

Your mind is not acutely focused now. Perhaps you have washed with soap; used shampoo, but you have not enjoyed the smell of the soap. You have not enjoyed the hot water in your muscles. You have not appreciated the refreshing clean of your hair.

The same happens as you continue your morning routines, getting coffee or breakfast, but not observing it, not appreciating it, not even disliking it, and desiring something else. This continues throughout the day. The momentum of overthinking every scenario fills your mind and dictates your actions. Alternatively, really, your lack of action. You, therefore, consistently find yourself in the past or the future mentally and emotionally and never in the present moment of life.

Why?

In many cases, an individual may feel a fear of living in the moment. This is often because the individual has worked himself or herself into a thought-place where they feel an overwhelming obligation to make sure the "now" goes perfectly. The individual may feel a fear of, essentially, messing up life or doing it wrong.

The individual has learned through one experience or another (or maybe several) that there is a great negative consequence if the moment does not go according to plan. A parent, a teacher, a sibling, or a friend may have taught this lesson, even oneself. An important and memorable moment did not go according to plan, causing a feeling of loss, negativity, or discomfort for the individual and likely others around them. The individual remembers this event, and with it, the negative feelings associated. The weight of making the right decisions is coupled with the negative feelings of the time it went wrong, and this is when the individual begins to overthink.

What initially starts as a thought process to help the individual safeguard against a situation going wrong, eventually deteriorates into a compulsive thought-behavior that is no longer serving or helping. In fact, it is very likely harmful or debilitating. Thoughts of doubt and second-guessing begin to occupy the individual. In an attempt to control and safeguard the situation as much as possible, the individual analyzes, then super-analyzes, every angle and direction.

Examining a situation to make the best decision is a beneficial thing- it has kept us alive, but here is the critical difference. An individual who analyzes a situation and then takes an action based on that critical thinking is practicing a healthy process. An individual who analyzes a situation but stays spinning in analyzation without taking action is not practicing a healthy process. In a sense, the individual has been rendered paralyzed by their indecision. The indecision is a result of staying stuck in the overthinking pattern. Does this sound like you?

Causes of Overthinking

It is important to understand at this point, that the subconscious mind works diligently to construct an internal map of reality. When something crosses our path, the mind analyzes the conditions and makes determinations; is this safe, is this beneficial, and so forth. The mind records this bit of data onto the internal map of reality. Our minds are collecting and recording data for our individual internal maps of reality all the time. For example, let us say you are getting a loan for a new car. You skim the contracts and agreements for the loan and the vehicle and sign all the documents. Months later, you realize you have been paying, and will continue to pay, additional fees you did not anticipate because you only skimmed the agreements. Your mind records data about this experience and plants it on your internal map of reality. The next time you are signing for a loan, chances are your mind will quickly recall this experience on the map, and you will not make the same mistake again. Instead, you will be safe and read everything thoroughly. In this case, the subconscious mind and your internal map of reality have served you well and protected you. That too is now recorded on your map, reinforcing what you know about reading contracts carefully. The more this situation occurs, the stronger the reinforcement becomes. This becomes your internal map; what you know and believe about your reality.

We can simplify this further with another example. Most of us have never experienced non-gravity. In fact, every day we have been alive, we have experienced and observed gravity, its effect on us, and the world around us. The idea that we will experience gravity's effects has been practiced for us greatly. Each of us has a very prominent marking for gravity on our maps. The idea that we would be able to move through our day without gravity seems preposterous. The map tells us that it is not going to happen.

However, here is the crazy thing: we are reacting to, and living by, the information on our maps, and not by the actual real world. Most of us have not gone through our day with zero gravity, yet some of us have. Some of us are dedicated members of various space programs and astronautics. These individuals have really experienced enough non-gravity in their days to have a much different mark on their maps about gravity. Our map says, no, you cannot experience non-gravity. However, in truth, it is that you do not experience it, not that you cannot.

The mental map of reality is a mental function we have adapted over hundreds of thousands of years as a means of survival. Think of one of our Neanderthal ancestors. He is catching fish in a stream, and a panther approaches. Our ancestor is unsure of this creature and suddenly experiences a great deal of danger, fear, and stress, but luckily comes away mostly unharmed. This experience is marked on his mental map. The next time our ancestor spots a creature like that, he can make the decision faster to move to safety, knowing what he now knows. I hope that this mark on his map keeps him alive longer because he knows the dangers of the situation.

However, millennia later, in the midst of the Roman Empire, another of our ancestors challenges his map. Even with everything he has ever observed or experienced about the dangers of giant wild cats, he declares, "I think I can take this creature." The map is challenged; the belief on the map is challenged. Lion tamers are born into the world and have continued for centuries. The internal map of reality for a lion tamer has a little bit different a mark than perhaps the average person. A first-time encounter with a wild animal does not generally make us think we can take it. Our map is much more heavily marked with the survival etch. However, we do know that some people are able to dominate a wild animal to drive it away, and we know some people make careers of taming wild animals. Therefore, that possibility is more real on our map than say, zero gravity.

Our observations and our experiences change our maps. Most importantly, it is challenging our individual map, challenging the belief on the map that expands our map. The mind naturally wants to expand the map and gather as much information as possible. You can give your mind the healthy activity it wants, by replacing habits of overthinking with positive and deliberate thinking.

So what caused you to develop this unhealthy thought process? What causes us to overthink and overanalyze the data on our maps?

There was a time when you did not feel this way, even if it was as a child. Try to recall a moment when you were thought-free and just enjoying the moment. A concert, a nap, a walk through a spring garden, watching animals or children at play, reading, watching a favorite movie, driving with the music up loud, spending time by the water, spending time with someone, just living in the moment. Free from critical and analytical thought. Your senses focused acutely on the present experience, the smell of the air, the perfection of the scenery, the pleasure of the company, the wind in your hair. You are capable of being worry-free and in the moment. You just need more practice.

You have been practicing a particular pattern of negative thought for so long that you are well versed at performing it. It may have served you once, but it no longer does. In fact, that well-practiced path is likely harming you in ways you may not even realize, both emotionally and physiologically.

As responsibilities begin to build on us, and we are weighed down with financial stress, family worries, and emotional trauma, our mind develops the habit of analyzing the situation for the best possible outcomes and worst-case scenarios. These are practically infinite, and as the imagination entertains each new river of possibility, tributaries, subtopics, side-questions arise, and more of those. The mind, in a way, can become addicted to following these little story-scenarios. In fact, following them so much that it keeps the individual from making a decision or moving forward. The lack of decision-making and general activity now allows time for the mind to again follow dangerously hypnotic tributaries. Why is it some of us don't get distracted by the tributaries?

We have practiced thoughts repeatedly that reflect self-doubt, worry and anxiety, self-critical beliefs, and a lack of self-confidence. We panic and freeze because of a fear that we are going to do something wrong, make the wrong choice, or say the wrong thing. The fear of this causes us to again follow the negative tributaries. The fantasy scenarios we concoct, keep us repeating the story in our mind. This practiced thought we keep thinking becomes a belief, and soon, the mind believes the story that we will fail, more than the story of us winning, simply because the fear of it kept us repeating the dreadful fantasy repeatedly. It is not uncommon for those who overthink, to develop a fear of the now moment and to do it wrong, so rather than confront the now moment, they hide from it in their minds and busy themselves with overanalyzing, under the guise of taking action. The choice to retreat to one's inner mind rather than face the circumstance is the comfortable choice because it is the well-practiced choice. Rather than risk the consequence and reward of the situation, the over-thinker creates a pseudo-moment in mind, many of them, as a distraction from making an ultimate decision or taking decisive action.

As overthinkers, we have essentially trained ourselves to think this way and to believe this way. These are the well-tread paths on our maps. However, if the internal map of reality can be expanded and changed, indeed, our thought-patterns and behaviors are also adjustable. If we have trained ourselves to think this way, we can untrain it, too. Our self-doubt grows, as we remain stagnant. It requires progress in some direction -any direction- to grow and gain positive and healthy momentum.

Defining Overthinking

In order to understand how we can correct the thought-behavior pattern that is no longer serving us as it is, let us take a closer look at what overthinking entail. You will generally find that the description of overthinking is to think about something too much or for too long; to worry and ruminate over a person, event, or thing. What is "too long"? When you come to the point that you know, a decision must be made, but you delay and dwell in worry or rumination instead.

The two major expressions of overthinking are worry and rumination. When you worry, you are obsessing over the outcome of a future event. When you ruminate, you obsess over the outcome of a past event.

This is you, driving in your car, thinking in your shower, lying awake in bed, thinking about what you might have said...what would have been the perfect response...what would have been the perfect last word...the perfect decision. What might have happened if you did it this way? The other way? Unable to let go of the past event and move on. Again, the avoidance of moving on by focusing on the past may manifest because of a fear of making another perceived "wrong decision" and suffering the perceived consequences of it, in the now. Alternatively, if you are obsessing over a future event, you are still avoiding the responsibility of the now moment, and the required decision that can only come from you.

There are common thought-patterns and behaviors that are often shared amongst overthinkers. Do any of these examples sound like patterns you practice?

- Reliving high-pressure, or embarrassing moments
- Asking a great deal of "What If" questions to yourself

- Spending a great deal of time considering the hidden meaning in words, posts, text messages, responses, email
- Rehashing conversations
- Reliving mistakes
- Losing track of surroundings because your mind is elsewhere
- Spending a great deal of time thinking about circumstances you cannot control
- Trying to not think of the thing makes you think of the thing more

In a clinical sense, the disorder of overthinking is noted by the extreme stress, anxiety, and fear of making a decision. Again, this is essentially a fear of making the wrong decision. Making no decision at all may have, at one time, been the better solution for you; it allowed you to avoid the consequence. However, you have likely come to a point now, when opting to make no decision is more detrimental and frightening than making the wrong choice. You realize you cannot continue with this pattern and achieve the goals and desires you harbor.

Though anxiety, fear, and doubt are often the side effects of overthinking, they can also be the cause of it. It is common for individuals with anxiety disorders and acute fears to resort to overthinking in an attempt to protect themselves. Of course, as we see, this behavior does not serve the individual but actually cuts him or her off from further progress.

Overthinkers seeking to overcome these negative thought behaviors eventually confront the idea of control, and of controlling one's environment and circumstances. The over-thinker wants as much control as possible over the scenario to ensure nothing goes wrong, but therein lies the problem, and perhaps the solution. We each, ultimately, have little to no control over the circumstances that arise, but we have full control over the ways we react to and manage them. Dealing with the idea of control, and thus the lack of control, allows us to face this realization and move us closer to the idea of letting go of control over a situation. Instead, we learn to trust ourselves to make smart and lucrative decisions for ourselves. Instead, we develop confidence in the moves we make, regardless of the result.

Chapter 3.   Typical Behaviors of Overthinkers

Now that you have an idea of what overthinking is, the next thing that you need to know is the signs of overthinking to look out for. Knowing the symptoms will inform you that you might need to be wary of the status of your mental health, maybe consider getting professional help. You can somehow gauge how deep into overthinking you are by identifying which symptoms have already manifested; if you find that you have signs of being a chronic overthinker, then you should probably consider getting professional help ASAP.

You Have Trouble Getting to Sleep

You cannot turn off your thoughts, even when you try; in fact, your thoughts actually start racing even faster when you try to stop them. All of these worries and doubts swirling in your head agitates you and prevents you from getting enough rest.

Overthinkers know the feeling of not getting enough sleep, almost too well actually. Insomnia happens because you have no control over your brain; you cannot shut off the chain of negative thoughts going through your mind at a hundred miles an hour. All of the things that worried you throughout the day come back just when you hit the sack, and you feel so wired that you cannot fall asleep.

If you are having difficulty calming your mind on your own, you can try different relaxing activities before you go to bed. There are plenty of things that might help you ease your mind just enough to let you get some sleep, like meditation, writing on a journal, adult coloring books, drawing, painting, reading a book, or even just having a nice conversation with a loved one. Do anything that can shift your attention away from the negative thoughts long enough for you to get some sleep.

You Start to Self-Medicate

Numerous medical researches have discovered that most people suffering from overthinking disorder have turned to use recreational drugs, alcohol, overeating, or other ways to somehow get a grip on their emotions. Overthinkers feel the need to rely on external stimuli because they believe that their internal resources (aka their minds) are already compromised.

It is never a good idea to turn to try to treat yourself from overthinking. Odds are, you will still be overthinking afterward, and you have to deal with a different problem brought about by your self-medication.

You are Always Tired

If you are constantly feeling tired, you need to take action. Fatigue is your body's way of telling you to listen to it because there is something wrong going on; you should not ignore it and just hop from one activity to the next.

Usually, fatigue is caused by physical overexertion and lack of rest. However, overthinking can also cause fatigue and exhaustion. Your mind is like a muscle; if you are constantly burdening it with dozens of heavy, negative thoughts all the time, and not even giving it some time to recover, it will get exhausted and cause you to burn out.

Back when humans were still living off the land, people did not have that many things to worry about, which means they do not have quite as many things to think about as well. In today's modern world, people lead complicated lives that require them to accomplish a lot of things in a short amount of time. In this fast-paced world, the need to slow down every once in a while is crucial for people's well-being.

You Tend to Overanalyze Everything

Overthinkers have one major problem, and that is that they always feel that they need to be in control of everything. They plan out every aspect of their lives, some of them even go as far as planning up to the smallest detail. They feel that doing this is the only way they can feel safe, but it always seems to backfire at them because it is actually impossible to plan for everything that will happen in their lives.

Even so, they still continue to plan out their futures, and they get anxious when unexpected things happen, and there always seem to be unexpected things happening all the time. Overthinkers hate dealing with things that they do not have control over; they fear the unknown. When unexpected problems do surface, they cause them to sit and mull things over instead of taking immediate action to solve the unexpected problem. Numerous medical studies have shown that overthinking leads to making poor judgment calls, which is why overthinking does not really help.

When you catch yourself just before you start overthinking, try your best to bring your thoughts back to the present by taking deep breaths and thinking happy thoughts. Before your negative thoughts go rampant inside your head, acknowledge them, and think about what they can do for you presently; doing this alone is usually enough to get rid of these negative thoughts because you will discover that their only purpose is to cause you stress.

You are Afraid of Failure

You fancy yourself a perfectionist, and you often think about how awful you would feel if you were to somehow fail. This fear of failure can be so strong that it paralyzes you, and it keeps you from learning from your prior mistakes, which often lead to you repeating them.

Overthinkers often cannot accept failure, and they will do everything they can to avoid it. Ironically, they think that the only way to not fail is to do nothing at all. They mistakenly believe that to avoid failure, they should not put themselves in a position to fail at all, which also means they are not in the position to succeed as well.

If this sounds like you, remember that you are more than just your failures; no one could even remember the last time that you screwed up, it's just you. Also, keep in mind that it is impossible to escape failure, and you should never avoid it at all. For failure allows you to grow and evolve.

You are Afraid of What the Future Holds

Instead of being excited about the things that you are yet to experience, your anxiety and fear of what could go wrong paralyze you into doing nothing.

If you are afraid of what the future could bring, then your fear keeps you trapped inside your own mind. Research shows that this fear of the future can be so crippling that sufferers tend to turn to drugs and/or alcohol just so they can tune out the negative thoughts that are clamoring inside their heads.

You Don't Trust Your Own Judgment

You cannot help yourself from second-guessing all of your decisions, from your outfit, what you will be having for lunch, or even what you will be doing for the day. You are always afraid that you will be making the wrong choices, and you often rely on others to reassure you that you made the right call.

Overthinkers, as mentioned earlier, are natural perfectionists; they constantly analyze, re-analyze, and re-analyze again, all situations that they find themselves in. They do not want to put themselves in a position where there is even a slight chance of failure. They do not want to make the wrong choice, so they take their sweet time making up their mind; they do not trust themselves enough to make the right decision for anything. They are so out of touch from their intuition that all of their decisions come from their brain, and this is not always right as there are times when you just need to follow your gut instinct. In addition, if your brain is bogged down from dozens of negative thoughts, it is hard to make a clear decision.

You Suffer from Frequent Tension Headaches

Tension headaches feel as if there is a thick rubber band wrapped around your temples, and it is slowly getting tighter. Aside from the headache, you might also feel a sharp pain or stiffness in your neck. If you suffer from chronic tension headaches, it is a sign that you are overworking yourself, and you need a rest.

And by rest, it also includes rest from mental activities, like overthinking. Headaches are a sign that your body needs to take a break; this includes your mind. Besides, you might not notice it, but when you overthink, you are actually thinking of the same things over and over again.

Overthinkers usually have negative thought patterns that loop around themselves. To fight this, you need to break this loop by reinforcing positive thoughts. Take deep breaths, and focus your mind on every time your chest rises and falls, being mindful of the present will help you get rid of negative thoughts and the tension headache that came with them.

Stiff Joints and Muscle Pain

It might sound far fetched, but overthinking can actually affect your entire body, not just your mind. And once your physical body is affected by your out of control negative thoughts, it will not be long until your emotional well-being gets hit too. Until you address and get rid of the underlying issues that cause you to overthink, the body pains will continue. Overthinking might start in your mind, but its effects will gradually creep into the other parts of your body.

You Cannot Stay In the Present

When you overthink, you will find it difficult living in the present moment and actually enjoy your life as it happens. Overthinking causes you to lose focus on the things happening around you, you are so engrossed at thinking about your problems over and over that it seems like you are trapped inside your own mind. If your mind gets bogged down by a ton of unnecessary thoughts, you are removing yourself from the present, and this can and will negatively affect your personal relationships.

You need to open yourself to the world around you; do not let yourself get too wrapped up in negative thoughts. The only thoughts that you should allow inside your mind are those that serve your well-being, ignore and forget about the ones that bring you down. There is so much beauty in life, and the opportunities for incredible experiences are unlimited; however, you can only appreciate them if you can manage to tune out the idle chatter in your mind and start listening to your heart instead.

Different Causes of Overthinking

Again, there is nothing wrong about thinking about your problems so you can think of a solution for them, it becomes worrisome when you have a bad habit of twisting narratives around in your head until you can see every angle and side to it. Overthinking is not productive as it just makes you dwell over your problems; you are not looking for a solution for them, and you are only making yourself feel miserable.

In order to find an effective way to break your overthinking habit, you need to find out what caused it in the first place. Below are some of the more common reasons as to why people tend to overthink their problems rather than actually find a solution for them.

1. Lack of Self-confidence

If you are not self-confident, you tend to doubt every little thing that you say or do. When you hesitate, even a little, about the things that you want to do, you are letting uncertainty and fear creep into your mind, and it will be very difficult to get them out of there. You can never really tell what your decisions will take you; even if you planned every little detail, the outcome will still not be what you exactly hoped for (it could either be better or worse than what you planned). This is why you should learn to take risks and not torture yourself when you did not get the results you wished for.

2. When You Worry Too Much

It is only natural to worry when you encounter new and unfamiliar things and events. However, if you worry too much that you cannot even imagine a positive outcome, then it will trigger you to overthink. This is problematic because worry attracts even more problems, sometimes it creates ones out of thin air, which causes overthinking to go even deeper. Instead of mulling over how things could go wrong, it is better to entertain thoughts that are more positive, like how much better you would feel if a certain even turns in your favor.

3. When You Overthink to Protect Yourself

Some people believe that they can protect themselves from troubles whenever they overthink, but the truth is that overthinking is a trap that kills your progress. Overthinking and not doing anything to change the status quo might seem good, but stifling your progress is never a good thing at all. In addition, when you overthink, you are not really staying in the same position, you are actually undoing whatever amount of progress you achieved thus far.

4. You are Unable to "Turn Off" Your Mind

Many overthinkers became that way because they cannot seem to get their minds off their problems no matter how hard they try. People who are sensitive to stress live as if they are constantly wound up tightly; they have somehow forgotten how to relax and change their chain of thoughts. Overthinking happens when a person stresses too much on a single problem, and he could not turn his focus away from it.

5. You are Always Chasing After Perfection

Being a perfectionist is not necessarily a good thing. In fact, one could argue that being a perfectionist is not good at all. Most people who struggle with perfectionism are constantly anxious.

They often wake up in the middle of the night, thinking of the things that they could have done better. Being a perfectionist causes overthinking because you are always trying to outdo yourself.

6. Overthinking is Your Habit

Overthinking is not always caused by a person's bad habits; sometimes overthinking IS the person's bad habit. For some people, it does not take much for them to overthink; they usually default to overthinking the moment that they encounter even minor inconvenience. This bad habit prevents people from living their lives the way they actually wanted to.

7. Reliance on Quick Fixes

With the advent of the internet also came a myriad of self-help videos, articles, and websites. The one thing that these resources promise is that they can help fix what ails you in a couple of easy steps. Of course, all of them are lying, but unfortunately, people usually have no other choice. However, there are many quick fixes that really do help, and that is the reason why it is problematic.

Are you hungry? Just order a pizza or Chinese takeout using your phone. You do not like walking? Get yourself a car. Do you need to talk to your mother halfway across the country? Pick up your smartphone and start a video call. The modern world has so many quick fixes in place for almost every kind of problem that people might have. However, quick fixes just work most of the time, not every time. When a person's problem remains unresolved for a few hours or even days, his mind automatically defaults to thinking that there must be something wrong, and this usually triggers overthinking.

For instance, if you are feeling blue or upset for a couple of days, there must be some kind of quick fix for it, right? You think you need to quit your job, break up with your SO, stop talking to your parents; yes, these things might provide some form of cure for what ails you, but are these the correct choices, not necessarily. These options are band-aid fixes, not really long-term solutions. And when these band-aid fixes eventually fail, people immediately fall into the spiral of overthinking.

8. Modern Life is Full of Chronic Stressors

When you feel stressed, the explanations that come to your mind are not the complete story. There are literally dozens of factors that might have contributed to your negative emotions, the things that you thought might be the reasons are just the tip of the iceberg.

For instance, when you feel lethargic, you might think that it must be because you are unhappy with your job, or if you are having problems with your family, it does not even scrape your mind that you need more sleep because you are just skipping one hour of sleep. However, lack of sleep actually stacks up, and if you skip an hour of sleep every day for a week, your body will reflect all of the stresses that you have accumulated.

It is like the myth of the frog placed in a pot of cold water that is gradually brought to a boil; the change in temperature is so gradual that the frog does not even try to jump out of the pot, and stays there until it is boiled alive.

9. Dreaming Has a Cost

Western culture respects and actually encourages people to pursue their dreams. This is not really a problem; it can be a positive actually, but when people believe that they can achieve their dreams with little to no effort, that is when things go bad. Most children grow up believing that they just need to be good little boys and girls to get ahead in life, but then when they reach adulthood, the magic vanishes.

Chapter 4.   Anxiety, Stress, Fear, and Negative Thinking

In order to treat your anxiety, you need to know where it is coming from. Many people describe it as feeling random. It might seem this way because the onset can seem to be out of nowhere. Overthinking causes and contributes to anxiety. They have a relationship to where they both feed off of one another. If you have anxiety, you have a predisposition to overthinking, meanwhile overthinking will increase your levels of anxiety.

There is a reason people who suffer from anxiety disorder are especially prone to overthinking. This is because their mind has become trained to think in worst-case scenarios. For example, they might be driving, and if they feel the bumps that sometimes happen when you're out on the road, and their mind goes to the idea that they hit something. Let me reassure you of something. You would not think you might have hit something or someone. The impact would be like no other. Not everything can be prevented because things happen sometimes. Still, as long as you are looking at the road ahead of you and do not have any chemicals in your system that could impede your cognitive function, it is unlikely that you are going to get into any serious accident.

Most of the time, it is not random when a person develops anxiety. Sometimes it comes as a delayed reaction of sorts. You might not feel the effects of it while you're going through a stressful situation because your mind is primarily focused on getting through the situation. After the fact, you go through the psychological effects of your situation because you have time to think about it. This is a common thing that happens to people during stressful situations. We stuff our feelings about it because we want to focus on thinking pragmatically and getting ourselves into a better place.

There have been findings that there are certain chemicals in our brain that can cause mood and emotional disorders when off-kilter. However, there also tends to be an environmental component. There are things that can happen to a person that makes them more likely to have difficulty handling stress. That lies where anxiety becomes a disorder. At a certain level, it is natural. When it passes that point and becomes a hindrance in a person's life, it has become a disorder.

Here's how it essentially works. You have an assignment that is due in two weeks. A healthy level of anxiety will make you think, "okay, I need to do this much work in this amount of time. If I want to make the deadline and put out good work, I can't wait around until the last minute. I need to do this much work every day to reach my goals." When it gets to be about the middle of the day, and you haven't done it yet, you start to feel a little uneasy and remind yourself that you need to get going. It's like a person inside you, giving you a nudge to get started on your responsibilities because they want to see you succeed. When an anxiety disorder takes over, you will be overcome with fear when you see the requirements and the deadline. You might think, "there's no way I can handle all of this. How will I come up with that much material in such a short amount of time?" Every time you begin to work on it, the blank page intimidates you, and you decide you'd rather spend your time doing something that does not cause you so much stress. Just the thought of working on it makes your heart rate go up. You tell yourself, "I can't handle this today, I'm going to work on it tomorrow when I'm stronger." Then tomorrow comes, and you use the same excuse to put it off.

Any number of things can cause an anxiety disorder. Everyone has times in their lives when their anxiety is at a heightened level. Major life events, such as illness in the family or the loss of a relationship, come with stress naturally. Even good things like getting a new job can cause anxiety.

One of the biggest reasons endings and new beginnings cause anxiety is because then the question becomes, "What comes next?" People have a natural fear of the unknown. Thinking about the new job, you might be confused because you don't know why you aren't jumping for joy. This might be your first job out of school, or it might be a major upgrade from your last one. The working conditions are better, the pay is higher, and your benefits are greater. However, you don't know exactly how this job is going to be. You might have read what will be expected of you in your new role, but that isn't the same as actually being in the job and going through the motions. You haven't met your coworkers yet, and you have only met your boss very briefly. You might have had to move for this job, so that means you're in a whole new environment. You're in a new neighborhood with people you've never met before, and you will have to find where everything is. You're hoping you don't get lost on your first day at work. Is it now becoming more understandable why you'd be nervous about starting a new job?

Sometimes anxiety disorders are born from trauma. When you think of trauma, you probably think of horrible assaults and natural disasters. While these would definitely be a source of anxiety, don't write off your experiences as not being enough to be trauma. If you had a parent who had a short temper and yelled often, and these temper tantrums didn't take much to provoke, it's easy to see where that would leave you with anxiety.

You would be unsure of your social interactions. You would interpret everything people do that seems off as a sign that they are about to become angry because you had been exposed to so much anger.

Thinking about the past can bring on anxiety. It can influence your future. Say you did poorly on your most recent exam. If you spend all of your time beating yourself up about it, you will actually be lowering your motivation to do better next time rather than increasing it. Every time you try to study for the next exam, your mind will go back to the last grade, which will distract you from learning new information. Your morale will be low, and that will decrease your self-confidence. People who do not feel good about themselves will not put in their maximum efforts in what they do because they do not feel that they will do well anyways.

There is no undoing the past. That is done. Acknowledging what you did wrong in the past should be an aid in doing better in the future, not an instrument to punish yourself.

The fact that you cannot change the past might be discouraging, but try thinking about it differently. If we could go back in time and change what we have done, which we can't, we would never be able to start a new beginning because we would be so consumed with fixing what has already happened. Then, what would be the point of improving as a person? You wouldn't have to because you could just turn back time and act differently, which might change the future in ways you wouldn't expect or want.

The permanent state of the past lifts a burden for everyone it places on us. The only thing we need to worry about is the present and how it will affect the future. Let's say you failed that exam because you spent a little too much time playing video games and too little time studying for it. You know what went wrong. Use the errors of the past in that way only. Use them for finding out how you got the undesired outcome so you can prevent getting a similar one later on. This doesn't mean you have a serious problem with gaming or that you need to give it up altogether. It means you need to find a way to incorporate it into your life so that it doesn't impede other aspects of it. Schedule the time you are going to fit into your day that is reserved for gaming and do not let it go past that. Make sure you have done everything you need to do before you start to do the things you want to.

Make a checklist for yourself about what tasks you need to complete before the end of the day. When you find out what material will be on your next exam, begin setting aside a few hours per day to study. If you have homework, get it done before you log into your game accounts. It can be tempting to start indulging in your hobbies when you get home, but there are a few problems with this. If you do wind up getting to your homework or whatever other things you need to do, you will probably wind up putting it off until it's nearly midnight. Once you get it done, it will probably be early in the morning, and then it will take you a little while after that to get to sleep. You will wake up the next morning feeling tired and groggy, and the work you did last night will have been done with a tired mind. Another possibility is that it will be nearly midnight and you'll decide you're too tired to do it tonight, and therefore put it off until tomorrow morning. This causes you to spend the next morning completing your assignment in a blur, and that is if you have enough time to do so and don't have to hand in a paper that has objectives that go uncompleted.

You will actually have more time to indulge in your hobbies and have more fun doing them if you do what you need to do first. If you have the fact that you have some homework you need to do while you are playing your games, the whole experience will be a stressful one because the thought is always hanging over your head- "When am I going to put away the game and get to my assignments? I'll do it right after this match. No, I'm just going to do one more, and then I'll get to it. Okay, I've got 4 hours to it,

I've got plenty of time. I still have three hours. I'll play for just a little bit longer. Oh no! I only have half an hour left! Where did the time go? I have to start now! Please let me finish on time."

The very stress of the situation will cause you to stay in your gaming and not tackle your homework. You think, "it's too stressful to think about doing that assignment, and this is relaxing me, so I'm going to keep doing it." However, you're not really relaxed. You can't be because you have a thought looming over you and nagging you in the back of your mind. The stress builds underneath because you know that no amount of doing nothing is going to make that assignment go away. In fact, the more time that passes, the more real it gets because you know you can only put it off for so long.

Keeping a schedule and sticking with it will take a very heavy weight off of your mind. It will also give you a sense of accomplishment. As you check things off your to-do list because you have completed them will make you feel more confident. When the list has been completed, you will feel good about yourself when you go to bed because you will know you have done everything you need to do.

Young adults often feel a great deal of anxiety due to social expectations. The way society is now; you are viewed as a child who needs to ask permission to do anything until you turn 18. At this point, you are seen as an adult in the eyes of the law, and now you are being expected to find out what you are going to do with your life. You've needed to go to your teacher for a bathroom pass, and now you're being bombarded with questions about what you are going to do in the way of a career. You go off to college, where you find out that you need to occupy yourself, and you also are solely responsible for making sure you have all your assignments done on time and know everything you will need to do in the near future. That has not been the case in the past. This is overwhelming. However, at least during your college years, there is a resemblance to your old life. Afterward is when many people find themselves feeling lost.

There is a growing problem following college graduation where people go through a period of not knowing what to do. They are struggling to find a job that is related to the field they got their degree in, or any job at all. This inspires depression, as well as anxiety. In fact, that is why it has earned the name "the post-graduation depression." Graduates feel depressed because they have nothing to do, and as a result of the guilt they feel for not having "launched" yet. It is also a time of great fear. You are wondering if you are ever going to be able to start your life. You may be feeling pressure from your parents to get your career started because they are looking at your situation using their own memory of when they were your age, not realizing the economy and society have changed since then. It is much more difficult for a person to get started with their life now.

It is also easy to let the anxiety about the future cause you to avoid thinking about it. Many people fall into the rut where they let days go by without job searching because it feels too stressful. In a way, it is a retreat into oneself. There are some ways to keep yourself from slipping into this and to get out of it if that's where you're at.

First, go to sleep at a reasonable time and get up early in the morning. When you are nervous about your future, you can find yourself in a habit where you fall asleep at a very late hour and then sleep until sometime in the afternoon. This is an avoidance tactic because then you can say, "Well, it's too late to go job hunting now, the day is almost over." You can' avoid your life. It will happen with or without you in the driver's seat. Set a certain number of job applications per day. Eventually, someone will say yes.

Also, think about exploring alternative career paths. For example, if you excel in writing, or just have an interest in it, you might want to consider freelance writing. You might choose to supplement your income with it, and for some people, it is their full-time career. It might seem impossible to start, but once you get that first client, you've gotten a foot in. Then you will find your second client. Most companies need a writer. You can be a blogger, a technical writer, a fictional writer, anything you can possibly think of; there is a niche for it in the writing business.

While you are searching for your career, do not beat yourself up about where you are compared to everyone else. You are where you are, and that is fine. Before you get started, use the time you have in between for self-discovery. Once you get into the workforce, it will be a consistent thing, so use this time in between for self-betterment. Feel free to try a few career paths before you settle on one. Think long and hard about whether this is something you could see yourself doing long-term. Do not beat yourself up about what you haven't done. That won't get you anywhere. Celebrate what you have done, and know that you are going to do more in the future.

Holding wasted time against you is pointless and will only lead to wasting more time. It is a road to nowhere. Making yourself suffer over a mistake does not undo it. Treat yourself the way you would a close friend who had made a mistake. You would not remind them over and over of the things they did wrong, and if someone tried to do that, you would probably stand up for them and tell that person they couldn't talk to your friend that way. Be a friend to yourself. Stand up for yourself and tell that voice in your mind it doesn't get to insult you, and you take it lying down. Let it know you will make up your own mind about yourself and that your self-esteem will have nothing to do with any unkind remarks it makes.

Chapter 5.   Clearing Your Mind

You know where some of the greatest overthinking causes are, you are working to slowly eradicate or reduce the issues that lead to information overload in your life. Now it's time to address the confusion inside your mind.

The concept of clearing your mind to be able to focus on the objectives of life or daily tasks has become very popular in recent years. Several authors and speakers have provided plenty of information and advice on how people can begin organizing, assessing, and then eliminating unwanted clutter from their minds. I agree that analyzing and knowing what is troubling your mind is an important first step in that process. That way, you will start connecting certain sources of overthinking with the thoughts that run through your mind. Cleaning up the overthinking sources is just as critical as eliminating the brain's individual thoughts.

Note that human beings are programmed to take information in and process it. Most of this information is stubborn, inducing emotional responses that can't just be pressed and dragged like on our computers to the recycling bin! Falling into a routine and making real progress in clearing your mind and learning how to manage and measure the importance of thoughts and feelings as you continue living, your life will take some time and concentration.

This journey is the beginning of a lifelong and life-changing process. Just because you are now discarding irrational thinking, it doesn't mean that in the future it will never try to creep on you again. Trust yourself and your ability to never stop moving forward.

So what do I mean to declutter the mind when I say it? Simply stated, there's no way you can start developing better habits and more positivity without first cleaning off the thoughts that hamper your progress. Most feelings and repetitive thinking patterns are connected to emotions that hold us back and even block our perceptions of what is actually happening. Many people take so much of the world's negative information that they lose all sense of confidence or respect for people, even strangers! Of course, when it comes to finding and forming real connections with other people, this is seriously restricting. Individuals who automatically start distrusting and disrespecting others will inevitably isolate themselves, leading to even more mental anxiety and depression.

The fact that loneliness and depression are related in many ways is attested to by most psychologists. Human beings, from the time we are born to the day we die, are social animals. For a long time, we are reliant on our carers. Once we become self-sufficient, we rely on others to work together to keep us alive. Society may look much different now than it did so many decades ago. However, from our relation and connection with other human beings, we still derive pleasure and an important fulfillment in life.

I mention those points because, I believe, a cluttered mind is certainly a form of loneliness. Speak of yourself as buried beneath an enormous pile of thoughts that actually have little impact on your life course. What was it that cardi b said this week? I should get the recipe I've seen on Facebook for that dinner. I can't believe that Drake has said that again. Is my tummy too big? How do I lose weight as do the celebrities? Was my boss angry at me for the joke I said at lunch today? blah, blah, blah...

Those thoughts may or may not ring any bells in your head, but I bet you will see a trend if you sit down and think really about many of the thoughts that keep coming back to you. You'll also see that in terms of your performance or progress in life, these thoughts or sequence of thoughts really do nothing for you.

In our view, many of these crowding feelings are examples of what marketers want you to think about. When you worry about something in your life or yourself so often, you may be tempted to buy goods that offer immediate improvement. Now we will start talking about a similar process, only that we are going to discuss the cluttered thoughts that are already in your mind.

Effects of a cluttered mind over time

The marketers are hoping to turn this negative emotional response into an incentive for buying their products to fix those problems.

So now, let's take a more detailed look at how a cluttered mind and information overload can have an effect on the brain over time.

You may have been informed that the new work colleague at the office, let's call her Jessica, boast about her brilliance in multitasking. She seems to fly easily through her tasks in a single morning and finish them quickly, while others find it difficult to complete one or two tasks before the lunch break in the organization. Jessica may get the impression that she gives her mind four, five, or even six different tasks, and her brain moves through all these duties in a timely and effortless manner at once. Okay, I just got to tell you. Jessica is just... wrong!

The human brain can just focus on one thing at a time. This is it. A person can learn to move with lightning speed from a thing to another, but he still concentrates only on one thing at a time. Basically, what a brilliant multitasker comes down to is, Jessica does a lot of things in a short period of time, devoting very, very little time to every particular job. Therefore, the problem becomes one of quality versus quantity.

This kind of rapid movement from one task to the next, depending on the type of job, maybe even a concentration that allows one to do the same work over and over without getting too frustrated, can be beneficial. Factory workers are required, during their shifts, to perform the same role again and again. To keep up with such a demand, you need a steady concentrated mind, or else he or she might dose off!

While Jessica appears to be doing a great job, the truth is that her "multitasking" raises her chances of making a mistake. When this happens, it can lead to personal frustration, because up to this point, Jessica has judged her performance based on how much she is doing — not really bothered about the quality of the work she's doing. Especially in today's extremely competitive environment, one error at work can lead to a lot of emotional frustration, which is brought home and turns into tension from one place to the next. This is a common symptom of a cluttered mind. This happens when you can't stop worrying about work, even if you are eating dinner with your children at home, then you're losing out on some of life's greatest joys— spending quality time with your children.

If you are, don't get discouraged. It is quite common, and there are certainly ways of handling this. But for now, let's cover some more explanations on why a cluttered mind is harmful over time.

If we lower the burden or remove this overload trigger entirely, we will begin to see how the emotions already in our minds are influencing us at present. Just think of it. How long ago did you become fascinated with this or that area of your life? If you have already found a cause of overthinking your childhood or teenage memories, the answer is a very long time!

When our thoughts ring back themselves and contribute to the chaos that is already filling our brains, it becomes more difficult to discern between what the good habits are and what is bad in terms of processing of thought. You would assume, for example, that a general attitude of mistrust, even at work, protects you against possible threats or risks. But look deeper and look at the flip side of that argument— what do you miss out on? And do you feel happy or unhappy about that attitude? Decluttering your mind is all about doing away with those thoughts that negatively affect you. The results can be mental, physical, psychological, etc. How emotions can do to you over time is breathtaking.

The harmful coping strategies

Most people who understand negative thinking processes but don't know how to deal with them transform into unhealthy ways of coping, which can lead to serious problems in health. Drinking, smoking, and illicit drugs are just a few of the most popular. How many times in a drama series have you seen the main character demonstrate she wants a cigarette to deal with the stress of a situation? Perhaps, after something terrible happens, a character who appears to have quit smoking sneaks out into the patio for a quick smoke. When it comes to dealing with a cluttered mind, these quick remedies do much more harm than good. It may feel so good to forget about them in the meantime, but they will never really go away without resolving your thoughts and behaviors, and you will need stronger and stronger measures of your coping strategy to send those thoughts away.

Another way that people try to run off their own brains is by coming home and tuning out in front of the television screen. It feels great to come home from a hard day at work and, instead of addressing the issue you've had with your manager or talking to your spouse on making a significant and stressful decision, you literally plop down on the sofa to binge on a Netflix series you've always wanted to see. Once more, the action is only preventative, not a remedy. Those problems will still need to be tackled once that binging session is over, even though running away for a short time felt good.

Yet, beyond just running away, think about the quality of a life filled with thoughtless, annoying behavior. What do you really grow towards? What are your intent and meaning? Definitely not vegging out eating junk food every night. Decluttering your mind means returning to your real-life ambitions, interests, desires, and beliefs. There they are, covering all the confusion inside. So let's make it clear so that we can get to the good part!

Let's declutter

The brain can perform just one task at a time, as I have said. So to analyze a group of disturbed thinking processes in your mind, we need to take some time to note down all those thoughts that we would find unhelpful, negative, hurtful, or irritating. Note, it's not always about just shredding a thought that negatively affects us — sometimes we need to weed these out and tackle them directly to dissipate their powerful influence.

Once you've got a list before you, it's time to take a look at each and feel how that thought affects you. The key to eliminating a negative thinking process is to commit to disrupting the thought whenever it comes into your mind. If you start thinking about that woman you think yesterday was flirting with your husband, stop the welling up resentment and ask yourself, "Has my husband ever given me a basis to believe he'd cheat me?" How often does he say that I love you all day long?" Would a dialog about the feeling get rid of the insecurity that I feel inside?" Most times, a brief conversation can be all it takes for profoundly hurtful feelings to be helped. Remember, it's your choice in life. If you really are in a relationship where your partner is continuously in question, then it is time to take the bold step on what to do about it. Before you agree, do not just wallow in intense grief for another ten years.

Looking at each item in your list, write down one positive feeling in another column next to it that would essentially eliminate the negative emotion-related to that bad thinking.   For instance, if you think incessantly about how well you're doing your job and fear you're not good enough, imagine achieving a challenging task and calling your supervisor to the office to applaud you.

Maybe it's hard to focus on good things happening all around the world because every source of news you read only talks about disasters. Do some research and check out for something amazing that's been happening in the world lately. It's not about downplaying what's happening in the world— it's about strengthening your mental state so you can get back into being a positive and satisfied person. Getting sinkholes sapping the positive energy in your mind is not beneficial for anyone.

If you get the hang of this method, go ahead and continue until you finish two columns in your list. The negative thought patterns are represented in one panel, and the opposite one covers an interrupting thought process to combat it.

I wish I could say that just writing down this stuff would automatically dissipate your cluttered mind, but you're going to make a commitment to stay mindful all day long so you can stop those negative or cluttering feelings. Some of those thoughts might just clutter your mind, not be linked to negative emotion. In this scenario, the interruption technique will be to completely disregard the idea when it comes to the mind. Finally, having eliminated sources of information overload should go a long way towards getting rid of the simple irrelevant thoughts.

Let me tell you, if you've tried to tackle all the cluttering thoughts you can think of in your head, you've certainly come a very long way from the state you were a couple of hours ago. At first, it may be difficult, but as you practice this routine disruption of cluttering and negative thoughts, you will soon begin to see the positive changes. It will become faster, and ultimately automatic.

Indeed the brain is quite versatile. Scientific research has studied the brain's trait, called neuroplasticity, in recent years. If you substitute negative thoughts with positive thoughts, the brain is literally rewired! Take that, Jessica.

Now that you start moving beyond the thoughts that had cluttered your mind for years, perhaps even decades, it is indeed time to move on to something much more interesting.

Finding your real goal, purpose, passion or goal

It's been defined in different terms in a lot of different ways— our purposes for living or the best part of living. We wake up every day for our thoughts or emotions or desires to pursue our goal. Maybe we get a lot of joy from practicing just a hobby. Whatever you want to explain, now is the time to begin to think thinking about how to fill that empty space, where your mind's cluttered thoughts once took root. It's time for a further exercise in thinking.

Think back to when you were a kid or perhaps a teen. Was there anything in your life that brought you childhood joy? Was there a sport or a talent or a hobby that you have been perfecting most or all of your leisure time? You may have enjoyed reading and just reading lots and lots of books each year during summer break. Do you enjoy diving, above all? Would you play basketball or baseball? Horse riding? Sketching and drawing? Maybe just chatting and laughing with friends was what you looked forward to doing each and every day. Whosoever it was, I want you to bring back the memory, if possible, to a time when you were doing all that you wanted to do. How did that make you feel like? Do you remember the joy that it gave you?

Most people struggle with this fallacy that when we become adults, the happiness that we feel in childhood disappears forever. This cannot be any further from the facts. Each of us still has that kid inside them, and once we reach a certain age, it's not a necessary phase of life that we abandon that. Most people have gotten a successful and fulfilling career from their childhood passions. We relive the joy that we felt every day as a child, only now, they get paid for it!

We don't have to give up being a child's independence of mind, playfulness, enthusiasm, excitement, all the most precious bits just because we are now adults. I'm not referring to trying to relive the past or become a child. What I'm saying is adults will experience joy and excitement just like a child. It is just culture and other cluttered minds that tell us there is no place for such things. Let's prove their point wrong!

Chapter 6.   Why Your Mind is Cluttered

Do you remember Mental Clutter? I explained that it is the condition when too many thoughts are racing in your head. In the words of Ryan Nicodemus, who has worked on Mental Clutter his entire life: the voices screaming in your head won't stop. The project that needs to be delivered at work. The family basketball you promised you wouldn't miss again on Thursday. The drama your daughter got a role in, and she's promised not to forgive you if you don't show up. The promotional examinations you were writing on Saturday and the list continues to go wider.

Every one of these things is in your head. You have made some mistakes with your kid, at work, and so on, and you can't afford to blow any of the new changes you got now. That is what we precisely call mental clutter. You would struggle to concentrate on one, and another pops up in your brain like a computer mail notification. In fact, you would skip your meals to cover up some of these problems, miss your pastime with your family and still find yourself in the problem. What to do? Trust me, I will tell you.

But before that, you need to view a complete list of the causes of mental clutter. Of course, you now understand that mental clutter is what causes disordered and excessive thinking. You will soon understand how you got stuck with this problem in the next few lines. This way, you can tell if you or someone close is already overthinking, and you can go on to pick the most applicable from a list of solutions I will be providing after.

Causes of Mental Clutter

You are scared of having no solution

Being scared is okay. It leaves a tingle of excitement mixed with eagerness in you. But you have to keep your fear in check. That is what most single mothers, double-shift working parents, and people who have superiors worry about. They knew they had to be home for the kids, they needed to be at their schools, and at that same time, they had to work out a rocket science at their workplace.

Most of the time, a client walked into my office and cried about making the wrong decision. I realize that what forces them into thinking out of width is fear. They needed to find a solution to their morass, and they hated the round of humiliation, sadness, and rejection that would follow if they failed. 'How do I tell my ex I needed to work the night shift and I won't be there for the kids, he's warned me he might sue for full custody of my baby!'. 'Who would stay with my frail Pop if I don't turn down the dinner invitation from the man I love, and how do I tell him I am not going to make it? There is a ton of tasks at work too, what would happen if I don't get them done?'.

Once you have more than one problem to deal with at once, there are very high chances that you would be obsessed with them, and you would be worried about failure. You would scan all the tasks in your head furiously and worry about being unable to find a solution to each and all of them. But why pass yourself out on the problems and their chances of failure or success? It makes more sense to take the problems one after the other and draft a list of possible solutions for them. The costs of failure or getting no solution would ring in your head and heart.,

You are engaged in obsessive thinking about the problem

This is an extension of the first problem I have shown you. I remember asking my secretary to stop working one evening. He had recently typed a paper, and it was replete with grammatical errors. That wasn't like him, so I called him in, and we sat at coffee. We talked about basketball, and I suddenly asked him, 'what is wrong, what are you worried about?'

'My wife wanted me to have a spectacular vacation with her in Australia,' he placed the teacup on the stool and focused. 'but I don't have enough, and I don't know how to get it.' I had to be home early because she was out of town, and the kid is too young to make his way back home from school'. I looked at him and sipped my tea. I listened like an audio recorder as he poured out his mind, then I stood up and patted his shoulders. 'Mike, do you notice that in all you have said, you have mentioned the problems you have, but you haven't considered at least one way out of any of the problems.' I watched his eyebrows crease in realization, that was right.

From my empirical research records, up to 35% of respondents in Prince of Edward Island agreed that they had problems, and they were so worried about the problems that they didn't think about the solutions immediately. The problems were in bulk; thus, they practically forgot they could solve them one before the other. If you are the type who gets obsessed with problems rather than solutions, 'there are ten big problems to solve at home and at home, where do I begin?' will be your famous rhymes. You would keep reciting the problems, and you may not be steady enough to sit and thrash one before the other. On the opposite, your igniting question could be, 'where do I start, which can be solved first?'

You believe overthinking solves the problem

This is the most ironic fact of the whole story. Perhaps due to the famous quotes we all read at college, a lot of us believe that the real solution to a problem is obsessing your life with it. Think and think till you find a solution. That may be right; an idea might pop in your head if you keep making your head work on a problem. But that has limitations. Nobody spends their whole life thinking about a sole problem. If you find anyone like that, you should watch them; they don't go far in life.

A lot of scientists who made monumental discoveries did not focus on the discovery their whole life. Whatever discovery they made was a part of the large research work they were performing. So, there is no reason to sit at work, at the dining, in your bed, at the spa, at the cinema and still think about the same problem.

A client, Nicole, once asked me after I gave her a similar suggestion: if I don't think, how do I get fast and immediate solutions to the funds I owe, or do I have to declare bankruptcy?' I understood her, and I smiled. She seems to believe thinking is the solution itself. She assumes if she thinks very hard, the solution would be in her grasp somehow. 'But what happens if there really isn't? Have you ever visited the psychiatry and met people who became patients for their wild imagination?'

Overthinking does not always solve the problem. If anything, it draws you away from your friends and families who might have better ideas if you mildly told them about the problem at dinner. If you can't trust their judgment, you should walk to a train station and talk to any random person at ease. You will be surprised that you could get meaning to life from something this simple.

You do not see a counselor

This is an important part that too many people don't take seriously. Statistical analysis reveals that at least 65% of citizens of the United States would not book an appointment with a counselor until things were awfully out of hands. They believe they had tight schedules, and fixing an appointment with a counselor could only steal out of their time. But there is the fact you are missing if that's what you think too. Counselors are like doctors. There is no perfection in the human body and soul, there is always causing you pain and worry in your heart, and there is still a health precaution you could use better. This is why one of your stable schedules must include seeing lifestyle and healthcare professionals.

If you maintain a stable schedule with your counselor, probably every fortnight or about, you could pile a list of things that take your time, activities that wear you out, problems you are worried about and share them all with your counselors.

A professional counselor can also read people; she can tell when someone is depressed, scared or thinking. "hey, you are moving a mile a minute, what's the problem?" a professional could tell you how you are feeling or how much you have been tasking your head the moment you get into talks with one. Right away, you would begin overthinking therapies too.

You are not paying attention to your health

How well do you consider your health? How often do you consider your health and wonder: is this really safe for me? If you had made it a full-time job to maintain good health, then there is a lot you wouldn't do now. You would practice simple workouts, healthy diets, no junks, timed break at work, et cetera. Believe me, you would practice moderateness in your thinking style too.

Let's say you are the guy who spends an extended part of his Saturdays in a basketball court, playing, clapping, and enjoying the thrill. There are Saturdays that things would get tight. That is because you probably have a lot more to do at work. So, you thought you'd better steal some time to get it solved on the weekend. You could go on and spend your weekend there. But trust me, your brain would not feel as relaxed as it often was on Saturdays. That may even affect the rest of the week. Now, you may be wondering, 'what should I have done then? If you ask me, you should risk playing what gives pleasure to your brain and watch yourself work like magic.

If you allow your brain enough rest, laugh, and have fun with whatever troubles you, an idea on how to solve it might suddenly drop in your head.

It is the same thing as eating. 'I can't wait for breakfast!' you would yell out to mom and jump into the taxi, your head already full of how you would resolve the day's problems. But that is absolutely wrong! Have you tried to compare how you work on an empty and how you do it when your stomach has had its fill? Don't even try to twist this; nobody works better on an empty belly! Whatever guarantee good health should not be toyed with, your thinking is healthier, more productive, and won't be shackled by hunger.

You are worried about time

Time is another problem people worry about. Rather than focus on the problem and its solutions, about 52% of women in Pennsylvania who cannot handle pressure are always concerned about time. Right, time is a factor that drives one crazy, you can't pause, you can't stop it, you can't even shout 'wait for a second!' and hope for anything. It keeps tickling towards the period the solution is expected.

The deadline for your enrolment and payment is a couple of days away. Your child's tuition is due. Your team has a big project that can turn everyone's face to your company. You are running out of time, and that alone is making you run crazy. You simply wish you could hit at something, someone, kick anything, and stop the whole madness! If there is more time, you could get one done and look forward to the other.

It isn't easier if you are just a staff member, and the team leader keeps yelling at you to move a quadruple your speed and turnout something huge. You would keep staring at the time, and your brain might start tickling the clock rather than the solution. This is why you must learn how to handle time pressure in cases like these. It is fine to check the time and see it tickling, but never should you let it tickle to the point of reflecting in your head and heart. Take your mind off it as soon as you can and focus on the problems at hand. I will tell you more about handling time pressure later.

You are getting emotional about the risks

This is one problem I hate to come across at work. It happens when you suddenly feel the pressure, the demand, and the urgency of the job in your body. The emotion climaxes in your brain, and all you would love to do is get the solution anyhow. If you have to choose between taking a mortgage and renting a flat, you might opt for a poor choice because you had a rift with your spouse and you want yourself out of their house immediately. I once worked with a manufacturing company that had a high market demand at some point. It was unusual, so they began to pressure their staff to overwork themselves within the working hours. 'faster! Faster! Move it, everyone!' you would hear each department manager scream at the top of their voice. It was crazy, and the manager's reverberating voice pierced into everyone's veins.

Regrettably, a lot of the staff members didn't handle the pressure well. Many became emotionally pressured, and they made a hell of mistakes. Many typists mixed what they were writing with what they are thinking. The machine operators mixed the wrong proportion of ingredients in the wrong order. It didn't take the managers long to realize that if this strategy were used, many people would have to be thrown out, or the company would run into a loss. Of course, the latter happened because the workers kept handling the pressure with a jumpy emotion.

At times like this, no counselor can do much for you because your brain and your body system are not relaxed enough to use anyone's suggestion. If you are the type who does this a lot, you would get home and begin to tell yourself by the mirror 'damn. I should have made three orders, not five'. You would sit at dinner and suddenly realized that if you hadn't been under pressure, you could have done something better. It is never okay to be under pressure, or worst, emotional disorder, and you must preach that to your body system every time you are about getting into one.

You have no definite plans, paperwork, and direction for yourself

Finally, we have to talk about you. What's your plan originally? Staying with Ma till you grow grey hairs? To leave for college and build your world there? To get married and never have a child? If you don't have a rigid plan from the start, you will keep getting into all sorts of problems. I will tell you that the first reason you were unsure whether to laugh or cry over your pregnancy was that you had no clear plans.

You would have known and prepared for it. It wouldn't have shocked you that someone is kicking you out of their house. You would also have been able to plan whether you would be going to see your daughter's drama, stopping at the dentist, or meeting the crediting firm on Saturday. Having a concrete plan saves you a lot of stress, time, and energy, assuredly.

Some people prefer to use the daily calendar, the phone reminder, or the room alarm to keep themselves working toward the plan. That is not bad, but what should work better for you is your mind. Train it to remember your plans. Note them down and pin them on a table near, board, or wall near. You would find it much easier to cross or substitute anything when unexpected assignments appear. With that, you won't get into a fit of emotion, thinking, or plans disorder.

You are demanding too much from yourself

This is an amazing fact that many people do not even notice about themselves. We recently examined the staff of three large companies. We identified the people who think more than necessary from our survey, and we obliged them for an interview. From their responses, we realize that most people had tasked themselves to produce more than what their bodies could. They wanted a great life for themselves. They wanted to put a smile on the faces of the people they love, and they wanted to get into the world on their own, free from other people's support.

These are all realistic dreams. But they are hemmed in a condition that makes it extremely hard for them to succeed, and as such, they would need the support they didn't want. They would get the high life they wanted but not at that spot, and they would require some time to achieve their dreams.

As a practical example, you would naturally overthink if you are always forcing yourself to think about the life you wanted but not getting. The cars you'd like to drive into your company someday. How you would love to try double shifts so you can earn more and show everyone you could do something. This is a very realistic dream. But you are against reality.

Chapter 7.   How to Stop Overthinking: Where to Start

A cluttered mind has no space for anything new. Often, when you feel that your mind is in a state of overdrive, it prevents you from enjoying the opportunities that life has to offer. Overthinking will put you in a constant loop since you feel like you can't stop yourself from ruminating over a certain issue. The worst thing about this is that there is minimal action you can take to solve the challenge that you are experiencing. As a result, overthinking only damages you as it holds you back from living your life to the fullest.

Learn to be Aware

Just like any other problem that you might be going through, the best way of solving it is by understanding the causes of the problem in the first place. With regard to overthinking, the first step towards dealing with it is by recognizing that you are overthinking. It is important that you live consciously by knowing what is happening in your mind. Any time you feel overwhelmed and stressed, you should take a moment to analyze the situation that you are going through. Your awareness should denote to you that these thoughts roaming in your mind are not helpful. Enhancing your level of self-awareness will help you stop yourself from thinking too much.

The following pointers should help you to boost your self-awareness.

Meditate

Today, millions of people value the importance of meditation. Usually, meditation stresses the aspect of focusing on a certain mantra or breathing. Meditating regularly increases your self-awareness since you connect with your inner-self in ways that you haven't done before. Meditation will help you connect with your inner self. Accordingly, practicing self-talk keeps you motivated on the goals that you have set for yourself.

Know Your Strengths and Weaknesses

Another effective way of increasing your self-awareness is by knowing your strengths and coping with your weaknesses. Undeniably, as humans, we are not perfect. The strengths and weaknesses that we have affect how we work towards our goals. In this regard, most people will only focus on doing the things that they are good at while doing their best to ignore their weaknesses. Knowing yourself better ensures that you don't waste your time and energy doing activities that will only make you feel negative about yourself.

Know Your Emotional Triggers

Also, it is essential that you know the emotional triggers that frequently influence your reactions. By knowing these triggers, you can catch yourself before overreacting. Moreover, your self-awareness can be helpful here as it guarantees that your emotions do not overwhelm you. Instead of reacting without thinking twice, you can stop to mull over a particular scenario and act accordingly.

Practice Self-Discipline

Every day, your life will revolve around things that you wish to accomplish. Achieving set goals can be a very positive experience. However, this doesn't come easily. You have to be willing to pay the price. This means that you should learn how to control yourself effectively and focus on what's more important. This is what self-discipline is all about. You should be ready to do anything that brings you closer to your goals.

Try New Experiences

There is a lot that you can gain from life when you learn to value the importance of new experiences. Think about it this way - the more you know, the more you find different ways of approaching life and solving the problems you are facing. Don't limit yourself by going through life with the same perceptions and doing the same things over and over again. Frankly, this will make every aspect of your life boring. So, go out and have fun. Try new things and challenges.

Motivate Yourself

We all need motivation at some point in life. When you are motivated to do something, your mind has the energy it needs to see through a particular challenge. Therefore, motivation warrants that you embrace positivity in spite of the problems that you might be going through. Indeed, this also has an impact on your self-awareness since you are surer about yourself and your abilities.

Get a Second Opinion

Earlier on, we had pointed out the fact that overthinking can be caused by overcommitting yourself. Maybe this is something that you are accustomed to. We all know how it feels when you manage to successfully complete a project on your own. However, at times it is important to recognize that you can't do everything alone. As you might have heard, "two heads are better than one." Save yourself from the nightmare of weighing your options on something over and over again. Just ask someone else for a second opinion. You will be surprised that you can easily solve a problem that once appeared too difficult for you. Therapy works in the same manner since you get an opportunity to talk over your thoughts with an expert.

Stay Positive

Instead of paying too much attention to the negative, change your thoughts, and reflect on all the good things that can happen to you. Savor these moments and help your mind adjust to the fact that you can also be happy. Develop a habit of encouraging your thoughts to stay positive.

Identify Distractions

There is a common phrase that goes, "what you resist persists." In line with the habit of overthinking, trying to prevent yourself from thinking about something only makes you think too much about it. As a result, the best way of stopping this is by doing something more engaging. Go for a walk with friends. Learn to play a new musical instrument. The point here is that you should make an effort to distract your mind.

Stop Being a Perfectionist

Evidently, there is a good feeling that comes with knowing that you have done something perfectly. Nevertheless, it is quite demanding to do things perfectly all the time. In your everyday life, you should leave room for mistakes. This ascertains that you will not be frustrated when something goes wrong. Focus on learning from your mistakes. Ultimately, you will notice that you start paying less attention to doing things perfectly. This creates room for more opportunities since you will be willing to try anything, whether you succeed or not.

Set Deadlines

Spending too much time thinking about a decision can lead to overthinking. Some decisions do not require you to think too much about them. They are simple choices that you can make within a short period. Therefore, it makes sense to set deadlines that you will make a specific decision before the end of the day. Depending on the importance of the decision, you should set ample time to ensure you end up making sound decisions.

Surround Yourself with the Right People

At times, it is difficult to think positively if the people you surround yourself with frequently have negative thoughts. If you spend most of your time with people who are always worrying, then you can be sure that you will also find yourself worrying. On the contrary, if you surround yourself with people who always think positively, you will also be influenced to have this perception about your dreams and aspirations. Therefore, you can help stop overthinking by choosing to spend time with productive and positive people. They will help free your mind from worrying about what the future holds for you. With their positive energy, you will appreciate the importance of living in the present.

Do Your Best

When facing new challenges in life, it is a common thing to see most people worry about what they can and cannot do. Unfortunately, this worrying attitude prevents people from handling challenging situations effectively. When faced with difficult situations, it is imperative to focus on giving it your best without thinking too much as to whether you got it right or not. You never know, there are certain situations when the outcome is not as important as you thought.

Create a To-Do List

We can attest to the fact that there are instances when the mind tends to blow things out of proportion. Have you ever heard your inner voice try and convince you that you cannot complete a certain project within a specified period of time? Frankly, this happens many times where the mind jumps to the conclusion that you have more things to do than you actually do. The funny thing is that the mind will even go to the extent of giving you reasons why you cannot complete the project. To prevent this from happening, you should learn how to work using a to-do list. A to-do list keeps things organized. It guarantees that you can handle one task at a time without making it seem too burdensome for your mind to tackle.

Cut Yourself Some Slack

The desire to succeed might be too ingrained in you that you cannot think of anything else that is not related to what you want. This leads to a scenario where you are too hard on yourself. You will find it difficult to forgive yourself for the little mistakes that you make along the way. Unfortunately, this leads to overthinking.

The truth is that you can't always expect that things will go your way. We are human beings, and therefore, we are prone to making mistakes. Successful people understand the importance of making mistakes. It gives them an opportunity to identify their weaknesses and work on them before reaching their goals. Imagine if people only succeeded without making mistakes. Mistakes should be perceived as a stepping stone towards success. As such, always remember that being too hard on yourself is damaging.

On a final note on how to stop overthinking, you should bear in mind that anyone can be a victim of overthinking. We all yearn for the best in life. Therefore, it is okay to overthink things from time to time. However, this becomes a problem when it develops into a habit, and you feel as though you cannot do anything about it. Your self-awareness, for example, will come handy each time you slip into a state of overthinking. Additionally, looking for positive distractions can encourage your mind to think about other things instead of sinking into your thoughts. More importantly, you should always remember to seek a second opinion from those around you. There is a good reason why we have friends and social circles. They should be there to help you offload thoughts and emotions that seem to weigh you down. Talk to your loved ones, and if there is no one to talk to, you can always engage in self-talk.

But you now know-how.

Having read this book besides having learned that overthinking is habitual.

You have begun to now understand that overthinking can come from a wide variety of areas in our life. Most importantly, how things like having boor sleep habits can affect and even make existing overthinking worse.

By understanding this problem at the basic level, you are much more likely to avoid encountering the many different issues that are associated with overthinking. See, because overthinking functions as a habit, it can seem at first very challenging to break that said habit.

But now you should understand how to break bad habits.

By eliminating things that have a negative influence on your life, you can further yourself. We all know that many things in our lives can have a negative influence on us. But trying to break this influence is often a challenging ordeal, many times we find that in trying to break a bad habit, we can sometimes end up developing a worse habit as a result.

This is where understanding the basics of habitual behavior comes from if you do not understand how a habit is formed and how it can play into overthinking you are going to be doomed to continue the process of overthinking. Knowing how a negative influence can cause you to overthink and how, as a result, your thoughts can begin to become cluttered allows you to take the high road out. When viewing overthinking just as anxiety, what can begin to happen is that you will get this black and white view of it.

This misses the many nuances that are associated with it, something as complex as our mind is not going to work in such a simple paradigm. It is going to be influenced by many different factors, and this is the case for something like overthinking.

Finally, with learning how meditation works, you now have the best defense against overthinking that you can ask for, a time-tested method that has been used by people all around the globe for generations to combat their anxieties and worries. That is what meditation is in the most simple and short definition; it is not some kind of esoteric practice; it is a simple calming method. With all of these tools now at your disposal, you are better prepared than ever to combat against overthinking.

Chapter 8. How to Stop Overthinking with Mindfulness Meditation

Life today is filled with lots of noise. Every day you have to overcome many forms of distractions from the digital space and the world around you. Before rushing to work, you might want to spend a few minutes checking your emails to see whether your project proposal was accepted. While driving to work, you have to control yourself from getting mad over reckless drivers while in traffic. That's not all, after sitting down in the office and getting ready to begin working, your notifications go off, and you're tempted to check your social media pages and look at what your friends are saying. Undeniably, the digital world we live in today is full of noise. Accordingly, it makes it difficult for people to find some time and sit in silence.

Unfortunately, the clutter that we have to deal with regularly prevents us from thinking clearly. It prevents us from making important decisions that could help to free our minds from worry. For instance, instead of working on your assignment, you might be distracted and waste a lot of time on social media. At the end of the day, you will begin stressing yourself over the fact that you might end up submitting your project late. Before you know it, you're overthinking about something that you ought to have dealt with earlier on.

Mindfulness meditation comes in handy as it can help you find peace within yourself and calm your mind. But first, let's understand what mindfulness meditation is and how you can practice it.

What is Mindfulness Meditation?

Simply put, mindfulness meditation refers to mental training exercises that train your mind to concentrate on your experiences in the present moment. These experiences are the feelings and emotions that you are facing now. The idea here is that you turn off your mind from focusing on everyday chatter and concentrate on the present. Practicing mindfulness meditation calms down the mind as you only focus on the present during the period when you're meditating.

How to Meditate

First things first, find a quiet place where there are minimal distractions. You can choose to do this indoors or outdoors as long as there is little noise coming from the surrounding environment. If you prefer doing this indoors, ensure that the lights do not distract you. During the day, draw your curtains and use natural light. Another important consideration that you should bear in mind is that you should choose to meditate when you're free. Don't do this when you are in the middle of something important. This can end up being a distraction, and it could prevent you from achieving the total focus that it requires.

How to Sit

Posture is an integral aspect of meditation. If you don't assume the right posture, you will find it difficult to meditate. It is essential that you assume a good posture that is comfortable for you.

- Sitting Down

You can either choose to sit down on a bed on a chair. Whatever option you choose, ensure that you are comfortable. When sitting down, confirm that your back is in an upright position. You can use a pillow to stabilize yourself and ensure that you're not straining to maintain an upright position.

- Positioning Your Legs

When sitting on the floor, cross your legs. Individuals who are unfit to do this should consider using a seat. If you choose to use a chair, make sure that feet touch the ground. Don't use a chair that will leave your feet hanging.

- Positioning Your Arms

Your arms should be comfortably positioned on top of your legs. The point here is that there should be no stiffness in the sitting position that you choose.

After assuming the right position, it is time to relax your body and mind. This is achieved by focusing on your breath. Pay attention to how you are breathing. Follow how you are inhaling and exhaling. Notice how your chest moves as a result of the air coming in and out of your nose. Pay attention to all bodily movements that you are experiencing. Feel the expansion of your thorax. The inflation and deflation of your stomach. To easily achieve focus, you can choose to count each breath that you take. A complete inhale and exhale can be counted as one full breath. Continue doing this until you reach a count of ten.

With time, your mind can get used to your counting process. Therefore, you could try changing how you count. For example, instead of counting from 1 to 10, count from 10 to 1. This creates more focus on how you're breathing and could, therefore, help you calm your mind.

Inevitably, you will realize that your mind tends to wander to other thoughts. This is normal, so don't worry about it. Recognize that your mind is wandering and learn how to bring it back to focus on how you are breathing. Remember, this should be done gently. Don't try to force things when you are in the process of meditating. You should be more aware of yourself and the thoughts and emotions moving around your mind. Therefore, you can manage how you think and what you think about it. Your focus here should be on one thing: your breathing.

Pay close attention to what is happening in your mind. Notice the thoughts and sensations that come and go. Don't resist them in any way. Just notice them. You are not required to react to these thoughts and sensations in your mind. Sure, they might be burdensome, but try to gently return to your point of focus without judging what you're feeling or experiencing.

As you finish, gently bring your attention to where you are now. Sit for a moment without doing anything. Breathe in gently and breathe out while allowing your body and mind to flow with it. Take another deep breath while gently opening your eyes as you complete your meditation. Stop for a moment and decide what you want to achieve within your day.

Mindfulness meditation practice is as simple as it sounds. Nevertheless, it's not that easy. Don't expect immediate results when first starting your meditation exercises. It takes time to master how to do it. Thus, you should aim to make it a habit as it strengthens your awareness. In time, you will notice the impact it has on you.

Mindfulness in Everyday Life

There is no law that restricts you to practice mindfulness while sitting on the floor or on a chair. You can practice mindfulness in your everyday life by being mindful of what you are doing. Below is a look at how you can apply mindfulness to your daily routine.

Washing the Dishes

Usually, most people will want to take advantage of the process of washing dishes to chat or watch a TV show. However, this alone time can be used to practice mindfulness. How do you do this? Immerse yourself in the process. Don't take anything for granted that is happening when you're cleaning the dishes. Notice the warm or cold water you are using. Pay attention to the sounds of the pans and other dishes that you are washing. Try your best to be present in the moment. Don't just wash the dishes for the sake of it. Wash them while taking the time to experience everything that is happening around you.

Driving

There are many instances where you may find yourself zoning out when driving. Most people spend their time thinking about what they did during the day. When driving home from work, some folks will use this time to think about what they will be eating for dinner. Practicing mindfulness can help you maintain your focus on the immediate environment around you.

First, if the radio is playing, turn it off. Alternatively, you can choose to play some soothing music that will help you meditate. While maintaining your focus on the wheel, practice breathing exercises as you pay attention to your bodily movements. Practicing this regularly can help prevent your mind from wandering.

Brushing Your Teeth

You can also take advantage of your daily routine of brushing your teeth to practice mindfulness. The main thing that you should pay attention to is your body. Notice how your feet are connected to the floor. Do you feel cold since you are barefoot on the cold tiles? Think about the way you're holding the toothbrush in your hand and how your arm is moving sideways or up and down to clean your teeth.

Judging from the everyday mindfulness exercises mentioned, it is evident that living mindfully is all about living in the present moment. Sometimes we find ourselves overthinking because we cannot control our minds when they are left to their own devices. Therefore, it is by being present in every moment that you can catch yourself overthinking and stop it.

How Mindfulness Can Help You Deal with Anxiety

When you learn to live mindfully, you will be more observant about what goes on around you. This means that your mind will be able to think clearly and identify situations or triggers that can make you anxious. The following are ways in which mindfulness can help you manage anxiety.

Connecting You to the Present

Mindfulness will draw your attention to the present. There is a huge benefit that you gain here considering the fact that overthinking tends to dwell more on how we perceive our future and our past. Since you will master more control over how you think about your future and past, you will be in a better position to prevent yourself from worry.

Mindfulness Retrains the Brain

One of the most important benefits that you gain by practicing mindfulness is that you can rewire the brain to think positively. There are new thought patterns that you will create through the exercises that you will be adopting. You will begin to appreciate what you have now and enjoy life without regrets. In doing so, you cultivate thoughts and beliefs that motivate you.

Mindfulness Helps Regulate Your Emotions

Mindfulness can also help you manage your emotions effectively. As you begin to enhance your self-awareness, you garner a deeper insight on how to control your emotions when dealing with everyday stressors. Your emotional intelligence will be given a huge boost. Accordingly, there are minimal chances that you will allow your mind to be consumed with anxiety.

Mindfulness Shifts Our Self-Perception

Usually, the beliefs that we hold about ourselves drives us to overthink about the things that we can do and those that we can't. For instance, if you believe that people don't like you, then you will fill your mind with self-doubt. You will never be courageous enough to argue confidently in the midst of other people. Fortunately, mindfulness shifts your perception as you will begin to believe in your abilities. Practicing mindfulness more often will have a positive impact on your life since you will be more compassionate about yourself and the world around you. The mere fact that you appreciate what life has to offer implies that you will express gratitude for what you have. This is a great way to perceive life from a positive angle.

Mindfulness and Healthy Sleeping

Besides helping you cope with anxiety, mindfulness can also ensure that you sleep well at night. By living mindfully, your mind gets the opportunity to relax. You will refrain from overthinking things and experiences that you have no control over. There is nothing that you can do about your past and certain aspects of your future. As such, it makes no sense that you should waste your energy ruminating over them. Mindfulness will, therefore, encourage your mind to live in the present, which will have a lasting impact on your sleep patterns.

When preparing yourself to sleep, there are several tips you should bear in mind to mindfully prepare your mind to rest.

Adjusting Your Lighting

You can prepare yourself to go to bed by adjusting the lighting of your bedroom an hour before sleeping. If the room is bright, you should adjust the lighting to allow for a more sleep-friendly environment. It is easier to sleep when the lights are dim. If you don't have lighting appliances to dim, consider using candles. The significance of doing this is that it soothes your mind to sleep.

Write a To-Do List

The quality of your sleep can be affected by thinking about the activities that you will be doing the following day. As such, you can free your mind from thinking about these tasks by writing them down before going to sleep. Craft a to-do list which details all the assignments that you will be attending to. Besides giving your mind an opportunity to sleep peacefully, you will also have saved time since you will wake up the next day with a better idea of how your day will unfold.

Remind Yourself of the Importance of Sleep

Sometimes, people forget the significance of a good night's rest. We tend only to remember this fact when we fail to get enough sleep. Before winding down for the day, you should take a moment to reflect on the importance of sleep. Express gratitude for the peace and tranquility that supports your uninterrupted sleep. This will quiet your mind from overthinking and help you focus on sleeping to get ready for the next day.

Mindfulness Exercises to Help You Sleep

There are numerous mindfulness exercises that you can use to enhance the quality of your sleep. The following are a few that you can consider incorporating in your daily routine.

One Minute Meditation

Just as the name suggests, this is a meditation exercise that will only take you a minute. Start by finding a comfortable place to sit. Close your eyes. As you maintain your comfortable and still position, scan through your body, and connect with the parts of your body. Take a deep breath as you continue scanning your body for any joints or muscles that want to relax. Again, take another deep breath in and breathe out. Follow your breath as it will help you become focused and aware. Just notice your fleeting thoughts and emotions. Take another final deep breath in and out.

Ambient Music

The idea of listening to music before you go to sleep can help you overcome insomnia and other sleep-related issues. When you find it difficult to sleep, this could be the resultant effect of your anxiety and nervousness. Listening to ambient music calms down your nerves, and before you know it, you're fast asleep. The following day, you will wake up feeling rejuvenated like never before.

Belly Breathing

Breathing exercises can generally help you relax. You should take the time to study how to do a full belly breath. Usually, breathing meditation involves regular breathing, and by paying attention to your breathing, you enhance your concentration. Given time, you will increase your self-awareness. This means that it will be somewhat easier for you to catch yourself when your mind is drifting.

In this meditation exercise, your first goal will be to be able to do a full belly breath. Start by sitting on a chair and make sure that you assume an upright posture. Place one of your palms on your belly and the other on your chest. Take a deep breath in and out. Pay attention to the hand that is moving. Certainly, if you're still breathing with your chest, expect the hand placed on your chest to move. In some cases, both hands will move. This will be an indication that you're still breathing with your chest. On the contrary, if the hand placed on your belly moves, then you have achieved a belly breath.

Practicing belly breathing is quite simple. All you need to do is the following: notice each time you feel anxious or stressed, and during this period, you should take a minute to take a few deep breaths while you pay attention to how your belly is moving. You can practice belly breathing meditation exercises without limiting yourself to a particular position. You can either do this while standing or sitting down. Moreover, you can do it anywhere, anytime you feel that your mind and body are not in a relaxed state.

Tension Release

If you're dealing with a challenging situation, you will likely carry troubling feelings throughout the day. Undeniably, this is a common thing that happens to anyone. When you feel emotionally burdened, it doesn't mean that you should give up on everything that you have been working on. Indeed, there are times when we feel like giving up simply because we cannot control how to deal with our emotions. Unfortunately, this affects how we approach our day to day lives. To be on the safe side, tension release meditation exercises can help you relax and find it easy to sleep.

Chapter 9. How to Stop Overthinking with Positive Self-Talk

Take a moment and reflect on some of the things that you have said to yourself today. Are you helping to build your self-esteem, or are you criticizing yourself for not being perfect? Self-talk is the inner discussion that you have with yourself. Evidently, this discussion can either have a positive or negative impact on your life. If you continue to talk to yourself about negative things, then there is a certainty that your mind will be corrupted with negative thoughts. On the contrary, if you engage in positive self-talk, you will increase the likelihood of building your esteem.

What is Self-Talk?

Self-talk is the inner discussion that you have with yourself. Everybody engages in self-talk. However, the impact of self-talk is only evident when you are using it positively. The power of self-talk can lead to an overall boost in your self-esteem and confidence. Moreover, if you convince your inner-self that you are beyond certain emotions, then you will also find it easy to overcome emotions that seem to weigh you down. If you can master the art of positive self-talk, you will be more confident about yourself, and this can transform your life in amazing ways.

You can't be sure that you will always talk to yourself positively. Therefore, it is important to understand that self-talk can go in both directions. At times, you will find yourself reflecting on negative things. In other cases, you will think about the good things that you have achieved. Bearing this in mind, it is imperative that you practice positive self-talk. This can be understood as pushing yourself to think positively even when you are going through challenges. When you do this, you will approach life more optimistically. As such, overcoming challenges will not be a daunting feat for you since you can see past the hurdles you are experiencing.

If your self-talk is always inclined to think negatively, it doesn't mean that there is nothing you can do about it. With regular practice, you can shift your negative thinking into positive thinking. In time, this will transform you into a more optimistic person that is full of life.

Importance of Positive Self-Talk

Research shows that positive self-talk can have a positive impact on your general wellbeing.

The following are other benefits that you can get by regularly practicing positive self-talk.

Boosts Your Confidence

Do you often feel shy when talking to other people? Maybe you don't completely believe in your skills and abilities. Well, positive self-talk can transform the perceptions that you have about yourself and your abilities. Negative self-talk can hold you back from achieving things in life. It can even prevent you from even trying in the first place. Unfortunately, this can drive you to overthink about the things that you feel as though you should do. So, instead of acting, you end up wasting your time overthinking about them.

Positive self-talk lets you put aside any doubts that you could have about accomplishing a particular goal. Therefore, you will be motivated to act without worrying whether you will succeed or not. You're simply optimistic about life. There is nothing that can stop you from trying your best when attending any activity.

Saves You from Depression

Overthinking can make you more susceptible to depression because you garner the perception that you are incapable of performing well. Frankly, this affects your emotional and physical wellbeing. Some of the effects that you will experience when you're depressed include lack of sleep, lethargy, loss of appetite, nervousness, etc. Positive self-talk can change all of this. It will fill you with the optimism that you need to see past your challenges. As a result, instead of believing that you can't do it, you will begin to convince yourself that you can do it. Positive self-talk can transform how you feel, and it's just a matter of changing how you perceive the world around you.

Eliminates Stress

There are many stressors that we have to overcome every day. The truth is that we all go through stress. The only difference is how we deal with stress. Some people allow stress to overwhelm them. Often, you will find such folks with a negative outlook on life. They will have all sorts of negative comments about life. "Life is hard," "I can't take it anymore," "I'm always tired," "Things never get easier," etc. We've heard such comments coming from our friends who have given up on life. The reality is that stress can get the best of you if you surrender. Practicing positive self-talk can help you realize that stress comes and goes. It is a common thing that everybody experiences. Therefore, there is no need to allow it to overwhelm you. When you begin to understand that you can change how you think and overcome stress, you will be less anxious and calmer. As such, this reduces the likelihood of overthinking.

Protects Your Heart

We all know that stress is not good for our health. Stress leads to many diseases, including cardiovascular diseases such as stroke. Therefore, by practicing positive self-talk, you will be protecting your heart.

Boost Your Performance

Positive self-talk can also help boost your performance in anything that you do. There are times when you find yourself feeling tired and depressed. For instance, when you wake up in the morning feeling as though you ran several kilometers, this can be draining. It affects how you attend to your daily activities. With positive self-talk, you can tap into your energy reserves and boost your performance. It is surprising how you can quickly change how you feel by thinking positively.

How Positive Self-Talk Works

Before getting into detail about practicing self-talk, it is important to understand how negative thinking works. There are several ways in which you can think negatively, including:

- Personalizing

This form of negative thinking occurs when you blame yourself for anything bad that happens to you.

- Catastrophizing

If you expect the worst to happen to you, then you are simply catastrophizing everything. The issue here is that you don't allow logic to help you understand that some things are not the way you think.

- Magnifying

Here, you pay more attention to negative things. In most cases, you will block your mind from thinking positively about any situation that you might be going through.

- Polarizing

You look to extremes when it comes to judging the things that are happening around you. From the perceptions that you have developed in your mind, something is either good or bad.

The importance of identifying these forms of negative thinking is that you can work to transform them into positive thinking. Sure, on paper, this might sound to be an easy task. However, the truth is that it takes time for you to live an optimistic life. You need to practice positive self-talk every day and in everything that you do. This is the best way in which you will develop a habit of thinking positively regardless of the obstacles that you are facing.

Tips for Practicing Positive Self-Talk

Have a Purpose

There is a good reason why you will hear most people argue that it is important to live a purposeful life. Undeniably, when you strongly believe that you are here on this earth for a good reason, you will strive to be the best version of yourself. You will be constantly motivated to try to achieve your goals in life. The best part is that you will feel good about your accomplishments. This is because they are an indication that you are heading in the right direction towards your goals. Therefore, when practicing self-talk, always look to a higher purpose that you yearn to achieve. This will keep you on the move without worrying too much about the number of times you stumble.

Get Rid of Toxic People

It is common to have a bad day. We cannot deny the fact that there are times when life seems difficult. Usually, this happens when our emotions overwhelm us. Despite this fact, there are people who have these bad days every day. They never seem to stop talking about their worst experiences. Unfortunately, this can take a negative toll on your life, especially when interacting with other people. Picture a scenario where you are always told about how life is difficult. Your friend keeps mentioning to you that life has changed, and it's impossible for you to realize your dreams. In time, this is the mindset that you will also develop. There is nothing good that you will see in your life since you can't think positively. The interesting thing is that you might actually be making positive changes, but you will unlikely notice.

Accordingly, positive self-talk will work best when you eliminate toxic people from your life. Sure, it might be daunting to let go of your supposed true friends, but if they can't change their mentality, then it's time to let them go. There is more to anticipate in life than ruminating on the worst that could happen.

Be Grateful

Positive self-talk can also take the form of showing gratitude to the little things that you have. Showing that you are grateful for what you have is a great way of changing your attitude towards life. For instance, if you were not happy about a certain achievement, being grateful that you achieved anything at all can help you develop a positive attitude towards what you achieved. The best part is that it gives you a reason to approach life with optimism. Develop the habit of expressing your gratitude every day. Start your day by writing down some of the things that you are grateful for. It can be as small as being thankful that you woke up. The point here is to tune your mind to focus more on the positive side of life.

Never Compare Yourself to Others

It is easy to compare yourself to other people more so when you feel that you lack something. Sadly, such comparisons only push you to look down on yourself. The comparison game will blind you from seeing the valuable qualities that you have. You will develop a negative attitude towards your abilities as you assume that other people are better than you. By expressing how you are thankful for what you have, you can identify the numerous things that make you different from other people. This is a great way of developing your personality and helping you believe in yourself.

Talk Positively with Other People

Talking positively with other people will have an impact on your self-talk. If you constantly talk about negative things with those around you, then there is a likelihood that you will also engage in negative self-talk. There are probably numerous times where you've heard people say that you become what and how you think. Therefore, if you keep focusing on the negative, expect negativity to flow through your mind. Stop this by trying your best to surround yourself with positivity, starting with the way you talk to other people.

Believe in Your Success

The best way of propelling yourself to succeed in your endeavors is by believing that you can do it. If you don't believe that you can do it, then this holds you back from trying anything. This should be applied to everything you do. For example, if you are working towards losing weight, you should convince yourself that you can do it. This is the first step that will give you the energy you need to overcome challenges on your way to success.

Overcome the Fear of Failure

Succeeding in life also demands that you should overcome the fear of failure. You should always bear in mind that your failures are learning lessons. In fact, most people who have succeeded in life have failed at some point. When you overcome the fear of failure, you will be more than willing to try anything without hesitation. This opens doors to plenty of opportunities. The good news is that you will have learned a lot from the experience of failing.

Use Positive Affirmations

You can also give a positive boost to your self-talk by using positive affirmations. The best way to use these affirmations is by writing them down. Note them somewhere you can easily view them. For instance, you can stick them on your refrigerator or on your vision board if you have one. The importance of positioning them in a convenient place is to guarantee that you motivate yourself every day. Ideally, this is an effective strategy of training your mind to always think positively. Examples of positive affirmations that you can note down include:

- I am blessed.

- I am a successful person.

- I embrace what life offers me.

- I am happy today.

- I allow myself to be filled with joy.

- I value the people around me.

- I am proud of myself.

- I am kind to people around me.

Avoid Dwelling in the Past

When you think too much about the past, it will likely be difficult to focus on the present. This will have an impact on your self-talk. If you keep regretting the mistakes that you have made, there is a good chance that you will think negatively. Your emotions will blind you from thinking clearly. As such, this can have an impact on the decisions you make.

It is imperative that you find a balance between thinking about the future and the present. When thinking about your future, focus on the positive. If there is something that you want, think in that direction and convince yourself that you already have it.

Recommended Steps to Changing Your Self-Talk

If you have never practiced self-talk, you might be wondering how you will start or what you will do to ensure that you change your negative thoughts into positive ones. The following are steps that you should take to change how you converse with your inner self.

Step 1: Observe Your Self-Talk

The first thing that you should do is to take note of the kind of talk that you have with yourself on a regular basis. Notice how your mind tends to think either negatively or positively or in both directions. While doing your best to understand how your mind thinks, recognize the effects of positive self-talk, and negative self-talk. This step should help you recognize the self-talk that you frequently have with yourself without changing anything.

Step 2: Choose Positive Self-Talk

The next step is for you to choose positive self-talk. Certainly, you don't wish to talk to yourself negatively. When choosing positive self-talk, this will be influenced by how you perceive things around you. Therefore, it is strongly recommended that you should begin looking at the bright side of things. For any situation that you go through, focus on looking at the bright side. Sure, you might be going through a tough time, but consider the benefit that you are gaining. For instance, it will make a huge difference if you learn something beneficial from the bitter experience you are facing.

Step 3: Recognize When You Engage in Negative Self-Talk

You can't be certain that you will always practice positive self-talk. Some situations will drive you to think negatively and, therefore, will influence your self-talk. Accordingly, it is important that you catch yourself when you notice your mind drifting and thinking negatively. Practicing this more often guarantees that you can shift your negative self-talk into positive self-talk and benefit from it.

Step 4: Manage Your Self-Talk

To transform how you think through self-talk, you will have to manage your self-talk every day. It is advisable that you manage your self-talk since there are times when you might forget its importance. Make a habit of talking to yourself positively every morning. Prioritizing your self-talk will warrant that you start your day on a positive note.

Step 5: Choose Self-Talk that Suits You Best

After practicing positive self-talk for a while, you will notice that some methods have a bigger impact compared to others. Use these techniques to keep yourself motivated throughout the day. You need a lot of energy to overcome your daily stressors. As such, strive to find the perfect type of self-talk that brings out the best in you.

Step 6: Eliminate Self-Defeating Self-Talk

An important part of self-talk is eliminating self-defeating self-talk. Negative thinking will exaggerate situations, and you may have difficulty solving challenging situations. The worst thing is that engaging in negative self-talk will only cause unnecessary stress.

Generally, positive self-talk can help you avoid overthinking. The basic concept behind positive self-talk is that you will develop a habit of focusing on the bright side of life. Sure, challenges will always be there. You can't avoid stress completely, but you will improve how you deal with stress. Don't think that positive self-talk is something that you can master in a day. It takes time for you to develop the right mindset required to see life from a positive angle. Therefore, practice positive self-talk every day, and you will notice its benefits after some time. To conclude, you should always remember that practicing positive self-talk is the best way in which you can constantly remind yourself of all the great qualities about yourself and the great aspects of life.

Chapter 10. How to Take Control of Your Thoughts

Like I said, social media has become the most common distraction that people deal with. We all know that technology plays a huge part in people's' lives. We believe it is also a reason for the problem of procrastination. But ironically, it has the answers to your procrastination habits. Since there is technology, you don't have to worry about ending your habit of procrastination. Why? There are numerous ways to overcome the habit of procrastination. Yes, for example, through motivation, you can overcome procrastination, but apps and tools sound more practical than motivation. Don't they? So, if you are looking for the best anti-procrastination equipment, know that there are many.

Small habits, big change

You already know small habits have a bigger impact on your life. For example, if you brush twice a day, you will not see the changes right away, but you will have a great set of teeth when you grow old. Just like that, when you practice simple habits, for now, there will be a massive impact on your life later. So, here are some of the tips that you should follow:

An organized individual

Do you think plans can't change your level of productivity? Well, try creating a plan, maybe for the work you have for next week or the work you have to complete tomorrow. And then, stick to the plan and see what happens. It might sound simple. You might even wonder if a simple plan can bring so much difference. Well, yes, it can! Through a plan, you organize the work that you have to do. When you organize the work, you understand the process clearly. For example, you have to complete a massive project, but if you just let the huge project be as massive as it is, you will not feel like doing it. You will not be able to see the amount of work you have to do in a day, and that will create boredom and ignorance. Thus, you have to organize the work that you have. Luckily, there are so many great tools and apps that you can find to organize work (more on this later).

Make it simple

Another common reason for procrastination is due to having complex tasks. Of course, some tasks can be complicated, but it is not as if you can't simplify them. For that, you have to set simple, achievable goals. Instead of saying, "I'll complete the project," say, "I'll complete the first part of the project today." When you make it sound simple, it will actually be simple.

Have a schedule

Once you have a goal, it is important to schedule it because scheduled work has a higher rate of achievement. Break your work into chunks and set a deadline. If you set your own deadline, you will be able to achieve them before the actual deadline boggles your mind. Sometimes, you might come across unexpected situations in life. Thus, completing the work before the deadline will help you stay in the safe zone.

Set aside distractions

You might already know the things that distract you. For example, if you are addicted to Snapchat, don't keep it your phone near you until you get the work done. Or, if you are a LinkedIn enthusiast like me, stay offline until you complete the work. Don't even add the Google chrome extension of LinkedIn because it is incredibly distracting. The moment you see the notification, you might want to check the messages even if you have so much to do. Thus, it is better to put all your distractions aside and focus on the work you have.

The Pomodoro Technique

If you don't know what this means, this approach promotes working for 25 minutes and taking a break for 5 minutes. Most people consider this as an effective and excellent solution for procrastination. Honestly, this is a fantastic technique, and you will be able to get a lot of things done if you follow this approach. Moreover, by following this technique, you can ensure the quality of your work as well. During the break, you must not get distracted, thus do something like listening to music, walking, or even screaming to release stress. Whatever it may be, make sure it makes you feel relaxed and comfortable. Thus, the activity that you chose to do should be something that you like, but not will divert your focus!

Reward yourself

I don't think anybody hates rewards, so it is highly recommended to reward yourself when you follow your plan. For example, if you set a goal to write 2500 words within 5 hours, you must treat yourself once you have achieved it! You can reward yourself with ice cream or an episode of your favorite show. However, make sure that you'll get back to your routine once you've rewarded yourself.

The myth of doing the hard thing

So far, you have probably heard that doing the hard things first, help you get other things done sooner. REALLY? Let me ask that again, REALLY? The rule of doing the hard things first don't work for me. If it works for you, then please ignore this point. But if you really give it a thought, you will understand the underlying concept. When you do what's possible, you become motivated to do the hard things too. Besides, when you try to the hard tasks and if it looks harder than it seemed, you might even delay the work. Thus, it is usually better to do things that are manageable first.

These are the small habits and changes that you must incorporate to become a productive individual. But there are many more anti-procrastination tips that I want to share with you.

Getting started technique

If you want to do something, you must get started. People usually procrastinate the beginning of a project, so it is important to understand the techniques to get started. How can you do it? Starting a project or a task will not be easy; in fact, it can be the reason for delayed submission. Whenever you plan to do a task, you need something to boost your mood. At first, getting started can be difficult, but when you move on with the task, it might seem possible. Thus, compare the way you feel when you start the work and the way you feel when you delay the work.

Even if you have done a little from the whole project, it's a good start. Starting the project is important, so it doesn't matter even if you do a very little portion of the whole project. There is a trick to make your mind like the work, and that is to start thinking about the work. When you keep your mind occupied with the task, you might somehow end up starting it. The reason is it is tiring to think, so you eventually start work.

For example, say you should edit an article. If you don't begin editing, you will never do it. Thus, just take the draft and change a few words. You will do it even without forcing yourself to do it, which is amazing!

Or you can set a timer. What can you do with a timer if you really can't start the work? Simple, set the timer to 10 minutes or less, and then, once the timer starts working, you just remain seated. Even if you don't do the work, just sit there. Eventually, you'll start work, and you will not even feel that you have started. This is an easy trick because when you are within your workspace, you can't help but work.

Thus, these tricks and tips might help you get better at what you are doing. The simplest mantra is, "get started!"

Useful Tools and Apps

Now that you've learned almost all the possible trips and tricks, it is time to get a grip on the tools and apps available. Beating procrastination will not be easy until you get help from the technology that you blamed for your reluctance. You have so many great tools and apps to select from, yet we'll discuss a few beneficial tools that you can rely on. Here we go!

Procraster

This is one of the procrastination-busting apps, but compatible only for iPad and iPhone. The app will support you throughout the procedures by providing the right answers and advice as to the option that you provide. For example, if you select the option "I don't know how to start," the app will suggest breaking the tasks into chunks. It provides not only ideas but also guidance to do the work. You'll find a rhythm to your work, and you can even check the statistics related to your productivity. The statistics will become a motivation to reach the goals.

StandStand

Anecdotally, it is considered that changes in the working environment can cause positive changes to your productivity. Thus, the introduction of the portable standing working table has become a great piece of equipment to fight against procrastination. Sometimes, you might get bored by sitting for long hours; in such a case, you can consider the StandStand table. The StandStand table helps to increase productivity by allowing you to alternate between sitting and standing at your workstation. Once you change your posture, you'd be able to do focus and get a lot of things done.

Focuswriter

If you want to type something on the laptop or computer screen, you must make sure that you don't get distracted. It is easy to get distracted when you have the option to open as many as tabs as you want. While working on screen, if you have too many tabs open, it will definitely kill your productivity. So, for that Focuswriter is a great tool. This is a program that works exactly like a Word document. It also has built-in timers, better ambiance, daily goals, and many other options. This program supports Windows, Mac, and Linux systems. By using this tool, you will be able to do your work on time with better productivity. Moreover, the time that you usually kill can be saved.

Freedom

This app provides peace of mind by helping you focus on the important things and avoiding distractions. Once the app does it for you, you will be able to focus on the work you do. People often procrastinate when they slowly shift from an important task to another entertaining activity. For example, say that you are working on a project, but meanwhile, you are scrolling through Facebook feeds, so do you really think that you can give your best to work? I don't think so. When your attention is divided among other unimportant tasks, you will not be able to give the best to your MOST important project. So, the Freedom app will help you by blocking sites such as Twitter, Facebook, and so on. The Freedom app will block almost all the time-consuming sites. So, there's no reason why you must not consider it.

Todoist

This is one of the popular apps that you might have often come across. People usually procrastinate because of not having a proper plan. Or not knowing the task to do next. If you have a structured plan, you will be able to understand the task that you must do next. So with the help of the Todoist app, you can get the structure of the plan. You can use this app to track and sync the tasks to your mobile and other devices. The app is available for Android, Windows Phone, iOS, and the web. Once you download the app to your device, you will be able to get the To-Do-List!

Write or Die

This is an excellent app for the ones who can't overcome procrastination even after changing their behavior. If you are still struggling to focus even after changing your behaviors, you must take extreme measurements. The app Write or Die will avoid procrastination by sending annoying pictures and sounds. This is called Kamikaze mode (derived from the term created from Japanese suicide pilots during World War II). When you delay work, the vowels on your documents will automatically be deleted. Perhaps, you wouldn't prefer deleting the words you hardly type. Thus this can be one of the best anti-procrastination equipment.

Spotify

This app will help you stay entertained while you are working. Whenever you find it boring to get your work done, you can play some great music on Spotify. This might help you avoid procrastination. Besides, if you play some motivational songs, you'll be driven to do the work.

Tomato Timer

I mentioned about Pomodoro Technique earlier, and this app relates to it. You usually procrastinate when you don't feel like doing a big task. But you still have to get this task done, and for that, you have to divide the big task into smaller tasks. The Tomato Timer app is the idea to help you to get things done by dividing them into chunks. You just have to set a timer, and then you will be able to get the work done.

Even though there are many more tools and apps that you can consider, these are treated as the most important and beneficial ones! Select the most suitable tool or app as per your preferences and make use of it!

Chapter 11.   Neuroplasticity: Regaining Control over Stress and Anxiety

Overthinking is a complex problem, but the solution to this problem is simple. To overthinking, you only need to stop thinking about negative things. Most people are fearful of the whole process of thinking. They find their minds in such a turmoil that they want to put a stop to the constant chatter in their heads. Fortunately, that's neither required nor possible.

One can only put a stop on the thoughts in your mind when it stops working completely, and by then, most definitely, even the person in question would also cease to exist.

A thinking brain is a good thing. An overthinking brain is even a better thing. We call people with such minds as geniuses. The problem begins when the mind starts to overthink negative things or the things we are not very pleased to ponder.

There is a possibility for the mind to think in the right direction or the wrong direction. Unfortunately, the mind chooses the wrong course, and that leads to all the problems. The solution to this problem doesn't lie in bringing the mind of a complete stop altogether. You simply need to train the mind to change its course and think in the right direction.

Before you start working on the solution, it is very important that you clearly understand the problem. Running in the wrong direction very fast wouldn't take you in the right direction. You will ultimately have to change your course of action.

The process will be slow, and you will have to be persistent. The mind can be very resilient. It will wield more control. But, in the end, if you show some perseverance, this problem can be corrected.

There are several ways to do this. From techniques to corrections, this book will cover all the aspects of getting over the problem of overthinking.

The first step in the right direction is to learn to control the mind. You will have to make some fundamental changes in your thinking so that you can come out of the cycle of fear and anxiety.

Overcome Mental Clutter

Decluttering of mind is essential if you want your mind to think positively. A mind cluttered with a thousand things will keep providing negative fodder. You may dispel one, though, and before it has disappeared, the new one will arise like zombies.

Mental clutter also makes you feel tied to things. You carry an unknown burden, and you don't know its worth.

For once, sit down and tabulate the things or thoughts that cause the trouble. Facing them is the only way to form a strategy to quell them.

Sorting the mental clutter is an important part of understanding the things that are causing the trouble. You must understand that it is not your mind that's causing the mischief. The mind is simply an amplifier. It will simply play the things that you put inside it. If you'll keep useless things ready to be fed into the machine, the product would never be as per your desire.

Putting the house in order is imperative. Every thought in mind cannot be important, and neither all the thoughts can be scary. However, if you don't know the exact number of scary ones, you'll fear everything.

Cut the mental clutter and find the things that you find really disturbing. Whatever is of no consequence should be pushed into oblivion. All your fears and insecurities should be clear in front of you.

Cultivating Optimism Through Positive Responses to Repetitive Thoughts

Fear and anxiety work as the fuel of negativity. The more you fear, the darker it will get. You can't fight fear with anger. Two negatives don't make a positive. The only way to invoke positivity is to cultivate optimism.

If you have failed twice at something and faced public humiliation, your mind would try its best to convince you not to try ever. It may start running all the humiliating moments in a loop. This can be disempowering.

The mind tries to convince you that you are not good enough at the thing you are trying to do.

Aggression, frustration, anger, or flight cannot be the answers. Your response should be that you are good enough, and you can do even better. This was not your best attempt.

There is a beautiful quote,

Failure is not the end of your story,

It is the beginning of your comeback story.........

In every aspect of life, your response to every stressful thought should be positive. This positivity would bring your confidence and charm back. It will help you in winning yourself back from your mind.

Negativity can push you in the dark corners of self-pity. You may have thoughts of self-rejection. You may feel that no one loves you or cares for you.

The fact is, even if you can't love yourself, how can you expect others to do the same. Love yourself. You know the positive aspects of your own personality. Explore them.

To fight extreme darkness, you don't need floodlights. Even a simple spark is enough to shake the empire of darkness. Always remember that darkness is fragile. It may look complete and overwhelming, but even a small spark of light can put a hole in it.

You don't need to find a whole lot to get over this blanket of negative thought cycle. Start with finding one thing that makes you lovable, and I'm sure that you'll be able to find many. You'll see that fighting the dark isn't that very difficult.

Cultivating optimism in your thinking is a winning strategy you will need to adopt.

Think Something New

There are some comments to which we have no comeback. The mind tries to lead us into things from which we can't recover. You may not find enough optimism to get over it.

So, do you surrender?

But, why do you need to play on the terms of the mind? Sometimes it's just better to sit and relax.

Diversion from a negative thought is the best way to avoid getting caught in the negative thought processes. If your mind is dragging you towards some really depressing things, try thinking of something completely different.

Think of something that really brings a smile on your lips. Engage in a completely absorbing activity.

This might look difficult at the moment. But, believe me, it is an easy thing to do. It just requires some practice and determination to break the unending loop of thoughts.

Find things that are powerful enough to distract you from negativity. It can be a hobby, your favorite pet, anything else you like to think about, simply think about those things when your mind starts racing towards negativity, and you'll find it easy to break the chain of thoughts.

Learn to Live in the Moment

One of the biggest problems of this age is that we have started to live in an autopilot mode. Most of the things that we do are habitual. When you do things out of habit, much thought is not required. You can still go on with that act while your mind is busy scheming something else.

This means the mind gets a lot of free time. There is a great amount of time when you are not using the mind actively. This is the time; the brain starts toying with thoughts.

We have made lives too easy and comfortable for ourselves. We also don't like to face too many challenges in conducting the day to day chores in our lives, and that helps in keeping the mind in the autopilot mode.

We weren't always like this. For our ancestors, the clear focus was a necessity. Lack of focus could get them killed. Nowadays, there are very few things that require such undivided attention.

Even while you are driving a car on a road full of traffic, you are doing a dozen things. You are listening to music on the stereo; you may even talk to a friend sitting beside you. You keep looking outside but not necessarily to navigate the traffic but to find something of interest. All this while, the mind can still be busy thinking about something that happened a week ago in the office and the response that should have suited the situation but didn't come from you.

All this is possible because we have got used to this mindless act of being in an autopilot mode. We forget that we are essentially a thriving life that was never meant to live the life of a robot.

We seldom pay attention to the things we do and say at that moment. Our mind does all the accounting later on and then reprimands us. The seed of overthinking gets sowed due to our overdependence on this habitual functioning lifestyle.

The moment you start living mindfully and pay proper attention to the things at that very moment, the cycle of overthinking that thing, later on, would come to an end as you will conclude the affairs at that moment. Hence, there will be no residual karma.

Mindful living is a good way to break the cycle of overthinking. It gives you better control of the mind, and you are able to think more clearly and judiciously.

Understanding the Importance of Perspective

Most of the overthinking process is a result of wrong identification. We feel identified to certain things in life, and that puts us in compartments. We begin comparisons from there and start computing the futility of our lives.

From the early days of upbringing, we are taught to have goals. We set life goals and then further subdivide them into milestones. A thing created for our convenience ultimately becomes our destiny. We remain nothing more than those goals. Our hopes, aspirations, joys, and deepest, darkest fears are attached to those goals. This is a big cause of the problem.

We set smaller goals for ourselves and then become too rigid on them. Smaller goals also mean that our perspective gets narrow. We find ourselves unable to see the grand scheme of things. When someone else tries to do something like that, we call that person a lunatic.

If you don't want some thoughts to completely overpower you, widen your perspective. Don't feel identified with smaller or inconsequential things that are limited just to you. Think wider, and you'll find that thinking about your problems wouldn't remain a problem. It is a good way to evolve out of the problem of overthinking.

Learning to Deal with Uncertainties

All things said and done, there is no way to eliminate all the uncertainties in this world. In fact, even this big blue earth is not immune to uncertainties. The creation of this world is a result of such uncertainties.

When we do something, there is no way to control the effect. At best, you can speculate the effect. There are always several external factors at play. However, when you have accepted the fact that there can be uncertainties on the way, dealing with them becomes easy. It isn't that the uncertainties go soft on you, simply you become more open to change.

Learn to live with it. There is no other way to survive.

Letting the Future Be

This is just the continuation of the point above. When you accept the fact that the result can be different from what you expect, it becomes easier to let the future be. You don't try to change anything and adapt.

You come out of the logical fallacy of grandfather paradox. Things in this world can exist independently. The cause of effect at one time may look significant, but it may not be detrimental in reality.

The best thing is to simply let the future be. Don't try to alter it as per your design. Adaptation is the right way to survive. There is no way that we could have come this far, changing everything as per our whims and fancies.

Don't Procrastinate Indefinitely

Overthinkers have a tendency to leave things for later. Their mind is testing things virtually, and hence they don't deem any physical action necessary. However, the longer you take to make a move, the stronger the grip of overthinking would become. If you really want to stop overthinking, learn to take action immediately. If you think that you'll give your mind the time of a day to get ready to take action and it would agree, you are wrong. It will find ways to convince you not to act.

The best way out is to take action as soon as possible. Action will lead to cause and effect, and you will need to respond, and hence you'll get past the stage of overthinking it in mind.

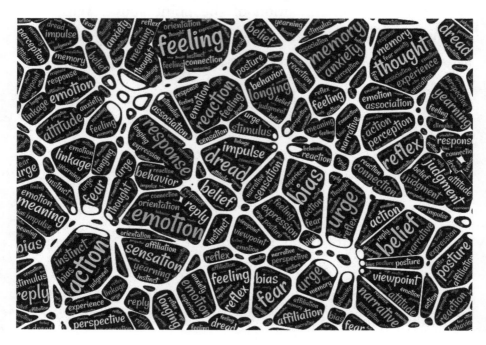

Getting Over Anxiety and Panic-Beating Overthinking at Its Best

The most common effect of overthinking is anxiety. It is a state of restlessness, fear, and angst that trips off the victim completely. A normally working person can start behaving in an uneasy fashion. It begins with slight discomfort and, if left unchecked, can mature to panic attacks.

The Signs of Anxiety are:

You feel your heart beating at an unusually fast pace

Your breathing becomes rapid

You experience lightheadedness

You can feel the butterflies in your gut

You start feeling visibly agitated

You start having irrational fears

It would be impossible for you to focus on a particular thing other than the thing you are worried about

You might even feel your muscles getting tense

There is a sudden restlessness inside you

There is something inside you that wants to avoid the things expected to happen

If you have felt these emotions, then you fully well understand what anxiety is and the kind of impact it has on the mind. Anxiety isn't a diagnosable condition. You simply feel its presence inside you.

Various things like your brain chemistry, environment, and genetics can contribute to the development of anxiety. However, your mental state will remain the leading contributor to the existence of the condition.

Three Brain Areas Playing a Key Role in Causing Stress and Anxiety

Amygdala: It is an almond-shaped area in the center of the brain that's responsible for invoking feelings of fearing and anxiety. This part plays a key role in the processing of emotions, and when you are feeling highly stressed, it invokes fear and anxiety as a protective mechanism. It senses the threats and alerts the brain to signs of danger. This is the part of the brain that responds to various anxiety triggers. For instance, if a person had ever had a drowning accident, this part of the brain would keep invoking the fear of drowning whenever the victim goes near a water body. The whole exercise is for saving the victim from drowning ever, but it is an escapist approach. The trigger can be any unpleasant episode registered in the memory of the victim.

Hippocampus: It is a complex brain structure that is embedded deep into the temporal lobe. This part of the brain is responsible for recording memories of all sorts, short-term as well as long-term memories. Memories of traumatic and life-threatening events, as well as unpleasant memories, are stored in this part of the brain. Problems in this area can lead to various mental disorders. Excessive stress and childhood trauma can cause the shrinking of this part of the brain, which can further complicate the issues.

Hypothalamus: This is a very busy area of the brain. It acts as the command center. It listens to various signals sent by the body in forms of hormones and chemical signals. It then communicates these signals in forms of hunger, satiety, fear, pain, etc. The fight or flight response felt during anxiety is created by this part of the brain.

There can be various triggers that lead to anxiety. A trigger is external stimuli that your brain receives through various senses.

Every individual can have different triggers for anxiety. There can be events, situations, people, or things that trigger anxiety.

Common Triggering Events:

Watching someone in agonizing pain, anger or a state of fear

Looking at someone resembling a tormentor in the past or having similar traits

A place with links to any traumatic incident

Any smell that reminds of you of the traumatic incident

Anxiety can have a paralyzing effect. The brain simply becomes defenseless. Escape starts looking like the best resort at that moment.

Anxiety disorder is one of the most common mental problems that Americans face. There are more than 40 million people currently suffering from anxiety disorders of various types. It is a highly treatable condition, but most people are never able to recover from it as they never seek help.

As explained above, if left unaddressed, excessive stress and anxiety can affect the functioning of the brain. It can shrink various portions of the brain and impair memory and other cognitive abilities.

Anxiety can impair the normal functioning of a person as an unknown fear stays with the victim forever. Uncertainty becomes a part of life, and people start shying away from unbridled public exposure.

Most things that lead to anxiety are not real threats. It is the mind trying to put you into a protective cocoon. There are several ways to counter stress and anxiety effectively.

Chapter 12. Overcoming procrastination

Now that you have accepted the fact that you procrastinate, and you have decided which type of procrastination you favor, it is now time to put the bad habits of the past where they belong—in the past. Procrastination is a bad habit, and now it needs to go.

Good habits and bad habits are created in the same way. Remember the baby learning to walk? The baby formed a good habit by doing something over and over; the baby used the power of repetition. We create bad habits the same way. You perform an action over and over until you have created a pathway in the brain for that bad habit's information to travel on, and now it is part of you. What makes habits difficult to change is the process that made them in the first place. The constant repetition has hard-wired that habit into your brain.

Habits are patterns of behavior that are formed by repetitiously doing the behavior. If you break the pattern, then you break the habit. There is usually a definite trigger that starts the pattern of behavior that ends with the habit happening again. The trigger can be set off by an emotional response or a response to something in the environment or something in the situation you are currently in. Think of going home after an absolutely awful day at work with every intention of doing an hour of yoga before eating a healthy dinner. When you walk in the front door, the first thing you see is the sofa and the television. Before you know it, you are laid out on the sofa watching a movie and eating delivery pizza. The sofa and television triggered a response in you that was based on emotion, situation, and environment. If you had entered the house through the back door, you might be doing yoga right now.

Following a pattern like this makes something a routine, and that is what makes a habit. And a bad habit is made the same way a good habit is. The brain does not differentiate between bad and good; it just knows that this is a habit, and it must be remembered to be ready to use the next time we see this trigger.

So, the first step in changing anything is acceptance. You have accepted the fact that you procrastinate, and you want to change. That is why we are here. Now we are going to put the past where it belongs—in the past. In the past, you failed to finish tasks on time. In the past, you did not always do what you were supposed to do. In the past, you were a procrastinator. But we are going to leave procrastination in the past where it belongs.

It is important to learn from the past even while you are leaving the past behind. All those negative experiences you had procrastinating will give you the information about yourself that you need to be able to learn and move on. Ask yourself questions about your procrastination to learn what you will need to go on to the next step. Think about the last time you procrastinated. How did it make you feel? Did it make you feel happy, powerful, excited? Can I use these same feelings to my advantage when I begin work on my new habits? Once you have spent a few minutes thinking about these answers, then we move on to the next step. Recalling the past for a few minutes is perfectly fine, but thinking about it for too long is just dwelling on it and does nothing for you but constantly remind you of past failures.

And now we change the focus of our energy to the present. Enjoying the activities of the present is one of the best ways to leave the past behind. Now is the time to begin on the path to the new you who does things when he is supposed to do them. Keep in mind that the things that caused you to procrastinate in the past are still present in your new future. You will still look at the same tasks and feel the need to procrastinate. This feeling will not go away overnight, but you will work toward correcting it every day.

The best way to stop the start of procrastinating is to be aware of when you feel the need to procrastinate. Sometimes it is quite obvious when we are procrastinating. We know if we consciously decide not to do something. We know when we say: "I'll do it tomorrow." But there are times when we procrastinate that we don't realize what we are doing until the day is over and we have run out of time. These can include:

Making lists

Doing tasks that are low in priority

Getting that second cup of coffee before beginning work

Leaving an important item on the to-do list over several days

Surfing the web

Re-reading unimportant emails

Answering unimportant emails

Staring out the window

Checking to see what is on television this morning

Gossiping with co-workers

Helping someone else with their work

Checking out the offerings in the vending machine

Reading the newspaper

These are just a few examples of how people manage to waste time. Some of them might be pertinent to you, and you probably have a few different ones to add to the list. How you procrastinate is not as important as recognizing you are getting ready to procrastinate so that you can stop the process. Beating the habit of procrastination depends on the type of procrastinator that you are.

Daydreaming Procrastinator

You need to look at the times you daydream and what you are daydreaming about to begin to understand why you daydream. Some people daydream to avoid a stressful or painful situation. This allows them an escape from possibly feeling negative feelings or thinking negative thoughts. Some people use daydreaming as a method of soothing their emotions. They can dream of their world the way they want it to be and create a fantasy world where life is beautiful.

So make a list of what you have daydreams about. Analyze the fantasies you create in your daydreams and try to decide what they are telling you. After all, these are your inner thoughts coming out in a short movie that you are creating. Do you see yourself somewhere else, geographically? Maybe you want to travel, or even to move somewhere else to live. Do you see yourself in a creative mode in your daydreams? Maybe you have a natural talent for music or art, and you need to explore that. You might be better at it than your conscious mind gives you credit for.

Think of the times you daydream and what you are supposed to be doing at that moment. Do you daydream of painting portraits when you are supposed to be paying attention in biology class? Your subconscious could be telling you that not everyone is academically inclined, and maybe your talents lie in artistic pursuits. Do you daydream about traveling when you are at work? Either you really want to go somewhere else, or this just isn't the job for you.

Understand what will happen if you continue to daydream when you are supposed to be doing something constructive. Can you accept the negative consequences associated with not paying attention in school or not performing your job the way you should?

Now pay attention to yourself and understand that certain things might begin to happen when you begin to daydream. You might no longer be able to remember the last thing that was said in the conversation. You lose physical focus with the environment by losing eye contact or leaning over to one side away from the group (think of the desk in school and your head propped up on your hand). When these triggers happen, break the moment so the daydream can't take hold. Sit up straight. Stand up and stretch if you can. Make eye contact with at least one person. Repeat in your head the last thing that was said. These are all techniques that will keep you focused on the task at hand.

Ronnie realizes that he most often daydreams at work because his entry-level job has become boring and routine. He still believes he will have more chances at promotions when he is lean and fit. Until then, he reads fitness magazines and imagines himself lean and muscular in his daydreams. Ronnie knows his daydreams are keeping him from completing his work when he is supposed to and that his daydreams are about what he really wants his life to be.

Distracted Procrastinator

The distracted procrastinator has little to no ability to focus on one thing at a time, no matter how important that thing might be. They get lost in thinking about the sheer enormity of the project or task and become overwhelmed by the number of parts involved. If this is you, then you will need to learn that the end product is not as important as how you get there. This isn't an elementary school math class where you had to show your work, and it had to match the teacher's version.

Your first step is to keep your goal in mind. See it in your head. Do you want to paint a picture? Do you want to find a new job? Do you want a clean, clutter-free house? By focusing on the finished product whenever you start to get distracted, you will begin to train your mind to not wander off just because this part of the job might be boring or stressful.

Now realize that you can't do everything in one day. It took Michelangelo years to paint the Sistine Chapel. Write down the steps you feel you need to take to reach your goal. Some goals may need fewer steps than others. Some goals are more urgent than others. If you are looking for a new job and you are currently working, then you are probably able to take your time and pick the job that you feel is perfect. If you aren't currently working, you may need to take the first really good offer and work that while you continue your search. It is all about what you need to make your life whole.

So pick one or two things that must be done every day to help you reach your goal and then commit to doing them. Do them first thing in the morning if possible, so you are doing them while your mind and body are fresh, and it helps to get them out of the way. If you are looking for a new job, check your email notifications while you eat breakfast to see if anything new has posted to the job sites you follow. If your goal is a clutter-free house, then make sure the breakfast dishes are washed and put away or at least rinsed off and put in the dishwasher.

And while you are keeping the end result in mind, try not to dwell on it. Most worthy goals will take a few days or weeks, or maybe even months, to accomplish. If all you can see is the goal at the end, either you will become discouraged and quit, or you will go back to procrastinating, so you don't need to focus on the goal. You need to focus on the smallest bit of work possible to work toward your goal at that moment. Eventually, you will find this is pretty easy, and you will probably do much more than your daily goal on some days. Just always hold yourself to doing the minimum and making sure it gets done daily.

Amanda is so fixated on the idea of a spotless well-running household that she can't focus on how to get there. So, Amanda has committed herself to two daily tasks that are non-negotiable. Every morning she will check the mail on the desk to see what bills are coming due and need to be paid. She will also empty the dishwasher and put all the clean dishes away, leaving the dishwasher empty for anything that gets dirtied during the day.

Defiant Procrastinator

The defiant procrastinator is perhaps their own worst enemy because they refuse to do anything; they don't feel it is necessary to be done. You know what your responsibilities are; you just don't want to do them. Some little inner demon is fighting a war with the part of you that wants to be responsible and is making you look like you are not capable of leading your adult life. Apparently, that way is not working as well as you hoped it would be, and you have become a procrastinator.

The key for you is to form a picture in your mind of exactly what it is you want out of life. Write some goals down on paper, so you have them handy to refer to whenever necessary. Now you need to commit to the idea that life is not all play, and there will be times you need to do things you don't want to do to achieve your goal. This is probably the most difficult form of procrastination to overcome because the problem is within you, not an external force that you can eliminate.

You will need to have a clear picture of your future goal in mind, and only you can decide if it is worth working hard enough to achieve. Then choose two activities that will help you get closer to achieving your goal and do them every day. Make sure the tasks are not so involved; they are impossible to do, and they do need to relate directly to your desired goal.

Brantley realizes that only he can get himself back on track and do what he needs to do to stay in college and on the soccer team he enjoys so much. He has committed to not missing any classes or assignment deadlines for the remainder of the semester. He will also speak to his professors individually and see which assignments he will be able to complete and turn in for at least partial credit. He realizes that unless he makes a good showing in college, he will never be allowed to enroll in law school.

Overdoing Procrastinator

If this is you, then you have a lot of decision making to do. You are trying to be everything to everyone. You are not able to say no to anyone. A part of you might feel like the world will fall down if you do not take care of it. But this simply isn't so. You will need to decide where you draw the line.

Go over your activities one by one so that you can see exactly how much you are involved in. Many people don't realize how many commitments they have accepted until they write everything down and look at it. Once you have everything down in a list, you need to look at your activities one by one and decide which is most important, second most important, and so on. Obviously, a full-time job or a full-time school schedule will take precedence over anything else. The other activities need to be ranked number two, number three, etc. until the entire list has a number associated with it. The first few commitments on the list are the most important and will need to be taken care of regularly. Everything else on the list will need to be analyzed by you to determine if it is really important enough to keep in your life. So pick the top two commitments on the list and commit to doing them every day, or as often as they are needed to be done. Do this for at least two weeks before you add in any other commitments one at a time, and don't add anything back in unless you really want to do that item.

Melanie made a list of all of her commitments and picked just the top two to do for two weeks. Obviously, going to work is the number one priority. She only works part-time since she lives at home with her parents and pays no rent. This leaves her time in her day to attend to her parent's needs, like driving them for doctor appointments or to the grocery store. All of her other activities are on the back burner for now.

Chapter 13.   Organize Your Life and Make It Simpler

Focusing on getting rid of bad habits isn't enough. Now, we need to introduce good habits into our new life.

I hope you've continued to work on the thought interruption for all those unneeded or negative thoughts. You've even come up with a new activity to try or go back to from when you were a child. It's time to focus on you as a person and what it is you want out of life. There are several things you can do regularly to prime your mind, body, and spirit for the new you. Let's look at a few of them.

Prioritize relationships with people—not things

In today's information-saturated society, it has become natural to pull out our phones whenever there is any amount of downtime. When you look at people waiting in lines all over the city, in stores, waiting to be seated in restaurants, they are always sitting or standing with their heads down, noses in their phones. And why not? On our phones, we can play fun games, chat with friends, read blog posts or news stories, keep up with our celebrities... Wait for a second, didn't we just talk about getting rid of information overload? That's right. Now, it is time to prioritize your relationships and interactions with other people. Let's set a small challenge for you to try this week.

When you go to the grocery store or to the bank, or maybe even when you take your family out to dinner next time, leave your phone in the car. What?! Yes, that's what I said. Leave your phone in the car. When you are standing in line—and this may be a little nerve-wracking—try saying something nice to the person behind or in front of you. I know...you might get a confused look, maybe they will be too immersed in their own phones to notice you, or perhaps it will have been so long since they've received real human communication, they won't even know what to do. But I challenge you. Talk to someone in line, then see what happens. Odds are, you're going to have a positive interaction that will stay with you for the rest of the day. Most people really enjoy chit-chatting with strangers at the store. A lot of people get a big boost in mood from even the littlest interactions like that. No matter how good it seems to feel when you get a new text or a like on your Facebook post, it's never going to feel the same as genuine human interactions. So, do yourself a favor and challenge yourself to connect with someone you don't know at least once a week.

Now let's concentrate on the relationships in your life with your loved ones, friends, and/or family. Think of one person who you consider a good friend that you haven't spoken to in a week or more. Why is that? Is it because you've been busy with work? Busy with the kids? For whatever reason, you've decided that other things in your life take precedence over your relationship with that friend. I would ask you to consider if you've really been too busy to fit in a 15-minute phone call with a friend. Perhaps you think you've been too tired after work and just haven't made it a priority. This is something I would challenge you to change in terms of mindset. Human relationships and friendships are the most important aspects of our lives, and it would be a shame to sacrifice valuable time with those people for a night of Netflix and pizza every single night of the week. I know work is exhausting, and you want to come home and just watch TV and forget about the world. But we've talked about this, too. Why would you waste away your life like this? If your job is so taxing that you can't concentrate on anything else and you are so desperate to get away from it that you can't function in the evenings, maybe it's time to reevaluate your career choices. But I'll wait until we get to that tip in a few minutes. Right now, your challenge is to set a date this week to go out and meet up with one of your favorite people for a chat and maybe dinner. If you don't want to spend money, invite them over to your place, and plan a meal together. Maybe you want to go over there because their house is quieter...that's fine! Whatever you decide to do, the important thing is that you set the goal of making time for a friend this week. This is a really great habit that you will get a lot out of. Much more than that pint of Moose Tracks ice cream in the fridge can offer!

Maintain that journal and track your progress

Journaling is a great way to keep your mind focused and record your progress. It's great to have a written source to come back to any time you feel like you need a little encouragement. Try to write a little bit in your journal every single day. Write about how you feel, what challenges you've succeeded with recently, and your determination to keep going. This is also a great way to keep yourself accountable. Write down what you've challenged yourself to do this week and write it down right away when you've completed it. Keep going, and soon you will have pages of great work to look back on when you feel you are losing steam or need a pick-me-up. Because we all have those days, and that's okay! Like I said before, this is a big undertaking. And it's important that your challenges not turn in to chores and sources of overthinking just like the ones you've worked so hard to banish! Challenge yourself, but don't over-burden yourself. I'm laying out several options in the hopes that there will be a few that really stand out to you, as something you think would drastically improve your daily life and your thought processes. And remember, no one changes their lives overnight!

Keep in mind that your journal doesn't have to just be filled with words. If you're like me and you enjoy motivational quotes or inspiring pictures, use your journal or notebook as a sort of scrapbook and include pictures, quotes, cartoons, even stuff like ticket stubs and birthday cards, stuff you might otherwise lose or throw away. These things are a lot of fun to look back on, and you will be happy you kept them later on.

Eat healthier

Eat healthier—not "eat healthy." I put it this way because there is no surer way to derail your progress than to overload you with a challenge like completely changing the way you eat immediately. If you are already a pretty healthy eater, that's great! But I would caution you and others alike to not get too caught up in any nutrition hype or fad that seems to be eating up your Facebook, and social media feeds. This is another great example of letting something intended to improve your life become a source of obsession, overthinking, stress, and feelings of failure. Nutrition plans and supplement marketing is just as big as any other form of marketing, and you should never adopt a diet or nutrition plan as the final say of nutrition. Use some common sense, don't overeat, and try to eat more healthy stuff than unhealthy stuff. That's really all you need to worry about right now. Don't go on an extremely low-carb diet right now. You're dealing with something far more important than that.

If you're wondering what a healthier eating habit looks like, I would suggest keeping a record of what you eat in a day for two or three days. For example, if you're eating frozen pizzas and cookies every night and notice you feel like crap, this could be a good reason why. I'm not saying eat salad and quinoa every day, but everyone can make one or two small changes to their eating routines and see a big improvement in overall energy and mood. Try to lower your sugar intake and eat a few more green things a week. That's all you need to do to start. Small steps, like anything else, will see you go far.

Exercise

It's time for everyone's favorite healthy mind/body tip—exercise! Now, don't groan. No, you don't have to start training for a marathon or buy a complete set of dumbbells for your new impromptu home gym. I've said it before, and I'll say it for nearly every tip on this list—one small step at a time. When you break things down and take it one step at a time, you will be far more successful with your goals than if you try to take on too much at a time. It is also so important, especially with exercise, to evaluate your personal condition and ability. Don't compare yourself with the YouTube fitness stars doing crazy workouts every single day and chugging protein shakes. This is about you and your personal improvement, and no one else's plan is going to match yours perfectly.

Just like with healthy eating habits, the first step is to take a look at what you are already doing and move up a rung on the activity level. That's all. If you're someone who enjoys working out but doesn't seem to find the time to do it, then I'm calling you out! Exercise is not about the length of time, it's about how hard you work, and I'm only talking a few minutes each day to start. If you are starting at zero activity, then your goal is simply to think of opportunities to walk or stand instead of sit. If you can, fit in a walk around the block or go to a park and walk a little bit. If you're at home, get up from your desk and do something physical every hour or two to get your blood pumping a little more. It's about making small changes. Turn those small changes into habits then concentrate on moving up another rung.

A lot of people think they need a pricey gym membership to get in better shape. This is just not true. There are tons of exercises you can do at home with zero equipment and little space that are adequate for improving overall health. Maybe you're a unique case if you're actually training to compete in body-building competitions. But most of us are going to see a huge improvement in mood, energy, and overall health from simply turning some of that sitting time into a little exercise. Search the internet or go on YouTube if you are unsure of what to do. Things like squats, push-ups, sit-ups, plank hold, jogging, walking, running, and dancing require zero equipment and can be done almost anywhere you feel like it. If you think it would motivate you if you had a partner alongside you, go for it! Go to a group fitness class every week if you think that would be more fun. The main goal is simply to add some physical activity to your schedule that amounts to more than you were doing before. Again, don't overwhelm yourself by trying to start a 30-day challenge or extreme 5-day workout schedule. Your focus right now is your mind—don't clutter it back up where you've worked so hard to find clarity.

Make time for you regularly

This is another one that can mean lots of different things to different people. Making time for you simply mean setting aside time every day to engage in an activity that makes you feel good and calm you. The exception I'm going to suggest here is that you don't make this chocolate or junk food time. Yes, chocolate makes you feel good...for a few minutes...but overall, it would be a terrible idea to form the habit of eating badly in the name of "you" time. I'm sure there are other, more healthy alternatives!

Do you enjoy massages? Of course, most people aren't going to get a massage every single day, but maybe once a month, you treat yourself to a professional massage. On a daily basis, find something that relaxes you and set aside half an hour or more just for that. Even if it's just taking a nap! Read a book, light a candle, do something that clears and relaxes your mind and doesn't work you up. This is about unwinding, but instead of replacing the stress of your day with something loud and distracting for the rest of the night, the goal is to calm and quiet your mind and body. Stretching is a great way to do this, especially if you've been stuck in an office chair all day. Maybe you just want to have a conversation with your partner or a friend over a cup of coffee. If you need to, brainstorm on a piece of paper before choosing something that speaks to you.

To-do lists

Many of us like to have every day organized, and that's great. The problem of overthinking creeps in when we start to obsess about getting every single thing on the list done, even those things that are not essential. Part of forming good habits is learning when to say no to something that you just don't have the mental energy to do if it is non-essential. If you feel stressed, but you're making strides toward changing your life and habits, then it's ok if you want to pass on that work outing or that birthday party for a friend of a friend you don't even know very well. If you think your time would be better spent at home relaxing or doing something you enjoy, then choose yourself. You don't always have to choose to give your valuable time and energy to others just because they ask for it. The obligation is a powerful force in a lot of people's lives, and many people end up feeling guilty if they don't always say yes to invitations or requests. But this is just another pile of clutter building up in your mind leading to overthinking. Feelings and thoughts of guilt are just as powerful as any other emotion, and you should protect yourself from them.

Organize your to-do list by priority. Obviously, grocery shopping to feed your kids comes before trimming the hedges in the front yard, and this chore should be further down on the list. Maybe make a separate list for things you need to accomplish today and things that need to be completed this week. This will give your mind a little more space and comfort. Instead of seeing a list of 20 things to do today, you may get to 5 or 6 things today, and the rest can be planned throughout the week as you have time and energy.

Ask for help when you need it

This can be a big one for those overthinkers who are also overachievers and perfectionists! Sometimes, we commit to too much, then feel obligated to push ourselves too hard to fulfill what we've committed to. Don't try to be superman or superwoman. There are going to be times when you need help, especially if you are juggling responsibilities with work and also a family. Have a conversation about it with your loved ones and friends, and you will find that most of the time, they are willing to help you out. It is important that you not feel like a failure asking for help. No one gets through life alone. Let this be an opportunity to bond and form fresh connections while learning to work together. You will feel much better, and your relationships will become stronger.

Be grateful

Clearing your mind of clutter is also about cleansing your emotions. When you begin to get rid of clutter and negative thoughts in your mind, as well as clutter in your environment that is connected to harmful emotions, it is important that you start replacing those negative feelings with positive ones. At first, it may take effort and a written reminder to get yourself going, but eventually, the goal is to make these thoughts automatic.

Gratitude is a powerful thing for the mind. It can instantly turn a stressful, bad day into something positive and hopeful. Instead of concentrating on the challenges you are facing and the things you don't have, think about all of the wonderful things in your life that you can be thankful for. Even the small things. Is the utility bill paid for this month? That is something to be thankful for. Do you have friends who care about you and that you have fun spending time with? Lots of people don't—so be grateful. Is your bed nice and soft with clean sheets? Look forward to sleeping tonight and be grateful. There are a thousand reasons all around you to feel grateful, and it is important to start noticing them, each and every day.

Gratitude comes with a lot of wonderful, warm feelings. It also forces you to refocus your mind on what's going on right in front of you and around you in the present moment. A lot of us get stuck in thinking about yesterday or the week before or even years before...then our minds shift to tomorrow and what's happening this weekend and next month and next year... How often do you just sit down and look around you and feel thankful for where you are in life? This is so important, and I hope you make this one of your top priorities as you build new positive life habits.

Chapter 14.   Conclusion

Now that you have read this book, you know that Overthinking is an experience playing repeatedly, and, more often than not, staying stuck in thoughts and things that have happened or are about to happen. Dwelling on thoughts that are not going away will generally affect the well-being of an individual, his or her normal functioning in life, and can result in the development of several illnesses.

Thinking is an essential part of the human brain. Research shows that while people can speak at the rate of 150 to 200 words per minute, they think at the rate of 1300 to 1800 words per minute. In that regard, thoughts determine people's destinies. Therefore, it is incredibly vital for people to choose the kind of ideas they allow in their minds.

Constant worrying, always expecting the worst outcome, and thinking negatively can take a toll on one's physical and emotional health. It can drain one's positive energy, leaving one feeling jumpy and restless. Excessive worry can also cause muscle tension, insomnia, stomach problems, and headaches, making it difficult to focus on work or school.

The correlation between worrying and negative thinking is a bit tricky because people experiencing this problem cannot determine whether worrying is making them have negative thoughts, or if those thoughts are making them experience depression.

Research suggests that positive thinkers enjoy life more than pessimists do. Actually, when it comes to physiological and psychological health, in addition to stress levels, optimistic people are way ahead of the game. Thinking positively is a good way to heal, so people need to understand that they should stop listening to the falsehoods their mind is telling them.

The endorphins that result from your activities work to improve your mood. A positive attitude, in turn, contributes to making a positive mindset. Once a person has a change of mindset for the better, he or she can manage worries effectively. Your mental health usually receives a significant boost from physical exercises. Incidences of anxiety and persistent worrying reduce over time. In addition, in case of a flare-up, you learn to tackle your stress or worry productively.

Mental clutter is mental overload, mental stress, or mental fatigue. This is anything that gives you anxiety, depression, frustration, sense of overwhelm, and anger. This clutter comes in the form of:

Regrets for past failures and regret for not doing some things that you should have done

Too many bills to pay and increasing debts as well as unfinished projects

Worries and insecurities

Inner critic

Feeling bad for failing to achieve something

Core values are convictions and beliefs that people adopt as their guiding principles in their daily activities. They are behaviors that people choose to exercise as they pursue what is right and what humankind expects of them

Examples of core values that emanate from the classification above include respect, honesty, freedom, fearlessness, dignity, loyalty, trust, cooperation, concern for others, initiative, justice, peace, humor, generosity, adventure, friendships, and excellence.

The next step is to follow the tips you have learned from this book and learn to live a good life free from worry and negative thoughts.

CPSIA information can be obtained
at www.ICGtesting.com
Printed in the USA
BVHW061408250221
601119BV00001B/243